CECIL ANDRUS

CECIL ANDRUS

POLITICS WESTERN STYLE

CECIL D. ANDRUS
AND JOEL CONNELLY

SASQUATCH BOOKS
SEATTLE

THIS BOOK IS DEDICATED TO THE GOOD PEOPLE
OF IDAHO, WHO MADE IT ALL POSSIBLE.

Printed in the United States of America.
Distributed in Canada by Raincoast Books Ltd.
02 01 00 99 98   5 4 3 2 1

Cover design: Karen Schober
Interior design and composition: Kate Basart
Front cover photograph: ©Dave Alexander
Back cover photograph: ©Stan Sinclair
Interior photographs: pages 8 and 170, ©Jack Williams; page 28, ©Dorsel "Mac" McClure;
page 46, photo courtesy of the Carter Library; page 66, ©Dave Alexander; pages 86 and
208, ©Barry Kough, *Lewiston Morning Tribune*; page 112, ©Morley Nelson; page 136, photo
courtesy of the Andrus family; pages 150 and 190, ©David R. Frazier Photolibrary, Inc.;
page 224, ©Stan Sinclair

Library of Congress Cataloging-in-Publication Data
Andrus, Cecil, 1931–
     Cecil Andrus : politics western style / Cecil Andrus and Joel Connelly.
         p.   cm.
     includes index.
     ISBN 1-57061-122-X (alk. paper)
     1. Andrus, Cecil, 1931–   . 2. Cabinet officers—United States—Biography. 3.
Governors—Idaho—Biography. 4. Environmental policy—West (U.S.) 5. Conservation of
natural resources—West (U.S.) 6. Environmental policy—Idaho. 7. Conservation of natural
resources—Idaho. 8. Idaho—Politics and government. I. Connelly, Joel. II. Title.
E840.8.A58A3   1998
979.6'033'092—dc21
[B]   98-13505

SASQUATCH BOOKS
615 Second Avenue
Seattle, Washington 98104
(206) 467-4300
books@SasquatchBooks.com
http://www.SasquatchBooks.com

*Sasquatch Books publishes high-quality adult nonfiction and children's books related to the Northwest
(Alaska to San Francisco). For more information about our titles, contact us at the address above, or
view our site on the World Wide Web.*

Contents

ACKNOWLEDGMENTS

No one survives the ups and downs of more than thirty years in public life without the help, encouragement, loyalty, patience, and commitment of many, many dear friends and a good staff. I have been fortunate to have had plenty of both.

I thought about trying to list everyone who has made a significant contribution, but I simply cannot. To do so would take another book. I am left to mention a handful who, without their help, this "political accident" would never have made it past the first reelection campaign.

First, of course, is family. Four remarkable women: a wife and three wonderful daughters who had to put up with a lot, and never, ever let me get too full of myself.

We have many dear and close friends, folks in most cases who are dear and close not because of, but in spite of, a life in politics. These are the folks who have us over for dinner and a few hands of bridge, or who share a duck blind or elk camp. They know who they are, and I hope they know how much they mean to Carol and me.

I have made lifelong friendships with the people who worked with me, the "names on the doors." Two guys pushed and cajoled me to work on this book, and despite that, they remain good friends. Chris Carlson helped me "feed the sharks" in Idaho and in D.C.; Marc Johnson served as press secretary and chief of staff in my second life as governor.

The Idahoans who went with me to Washington, D.C., were dubbed the "Idaho mafia" and no one had better lieutenants; people like Billie Jeppsen, Gary Catron, Joe Nagel, John Hough, and the late Larry Meierotto.

In the early years in the statehouse I had the help of a wonderful friend who left us much too soon, Ed Williams. Jean Taylor, Bill Murphy, Rollie Bruning, Pat Vaughn, and Merle Parsley all made a young governor look good.

When I made a return visit to the governor's office, I enjoyed the support of a whole new staff of eager and loyal Idahoans. Clareene Wharry was, and is, indispensable as a personal assistant. Mike Mitchell and Clancy Standridge were the gray hairs who provided the necessary seasoning for their younger colleagues Andy Brunelle, John Carter, Alice Koskella, Kevan Fenderson, Julie Cheever, and Scott Peyron. Every office should be lucky enough to have a Pam Parks, a Jody Taylor, and a Zuriel Knowles, who just may hold the record for longest continuous service to Idaho governors. Chuck Moss forgot more about the state budget than most will ever know. Darrell Manning did every job I ever asked him to do, and did them all superbly. The same is true of Wally Hedrick and Wayne Mittleider. Two Bobs—Lenaghan and Montgomery—were there from the beginning. I miss them both.

There are hundreds of others. Each has a special place in my heart, the kind of place possible only when people share great affection and common purpose. I've often said the very best thing about a life in politics, and this may be particularly true in the West, are lifelong friendships. It wasn't a bad run. Thanks to all who made it something very special for me.

—Cecil D. Andrus

I owe many thanks to three colleagues from the *Seattle Post-Intelligencer*. Our publisher, J. D. Alexander, championed this project from the beginning. John Nanney, of the systems department, provided indispensable technical help as chapters were composed on portable computers at various locales. Our national editor, Bob Schenet, made time available for the many Idaho travels involved in the authors' work.

Writing a daily story and putting together a book are vastly different tasks. My thanks to Timothy Egan, Northwest bureau chief of the *New York Times*, for sharing his writing regime. Our editor at Sasquatch, Gary Luke, was patient and affirming at all times.

I would thank my partner in life, Michelle Pailthorp, for her patience throughout. Our family's two black standard poodles, Norman and S'Murphy Brown, knew to take me on long walks whenever any questions needed to be thought through.

—*Joel Connelly*

HORNSWOGGLING ALONG

O NLY ONE LABEL CAN BEGIN TO DESCRIBE accurately what I am—a Westerner. The word refers not only to where I live, but to how I live. Although I've been a governor and member of the president's cabinet, I still spend hours in cold water trying to hook a steelhead or cutthroat trout, scramble around rocky hills hunting chukars, and love to think about the time I played hooky for three days from a gubernatorial campaign to bag an elk. Taking that time off nearly shot down my political career; I won the election by a margin of only thirty-six hundred votes.

Being a Westerner, in my mind, means enjoying the physical beauty of the land and appreciating the independence and plain speech of its people. It denotes the place to which I am rooted and to which I have always returned. After four years as secretary of the interior for President Carter, I was asked if I planned to stay in Washington, D.C., in some sort of power or lobbying position. "The only reason so many people live on the East Coast is they don't know any better," I replied. "I prefer the Western way of life, where people treat you the same way to your face as they do behind your back."

My wife, Carol, says she should have seen the warning signs of a political career when we were high school students in Eugene, Oregon. I ran for a whole series of offices, winning every time until I lost the student body presidency on the absentee vote.

I never planned on it, would never have dreamed of it, but more than half of my adult life has been spent in politics. Nor would I have dreamed how the West has been transformed from the days, back in the mid-1950s, when I went to work as a mill manager and lumberjack in Orofino, Idaho.

During the last thirty-five years, I've been involved full time in shaping change in the West. I'm a conservationist, and I acted on my belief that Idaho and Alaska offer the last, best chance to keep a chunk of the natural world intact. America's frontiers aren't always for the taming. At the same time, I was a four-term governor of Idaho who tried to diversify an economy that had sputtered through downturns in our traditional resource industries. As a college dropout, I was painfully aware that education plays a vital role in enhancing life's prospects, and that high-possibility jobs are essential to building a state.

I've been deeply involved in battles over habitat between humans and other predators. I gained accolades, and Robert Redford as a guest at my fund-raisers, for campaigning to save the grassland hunting domain of the eagles, hawks, and falcons that nest in cliffs along the Snake River south of Boise. But I was damned by conservationists for taking a dim view toward reintroducing the grizzly bear to the Bitterroot Mountains. I saw nothing for *Ursus horribilis* to eat, and inevitable rancher-bear conflicts that the animals would surely lose.

I struggle to find words to tell what I've done, why I did it, and where I screwed up. A good place to reflect, in Idaho naturally, is the 4,245-foot summit of White Bird Hill. It is one of the Pacific Northwest's most breathtaking and historically important spots, and a place that gives perspective. The hill looks down into the great canyon of the Salmon River, one of America's longest undammed streams, surrounded by untamed wilderness in which I have rafted, hunted, and gone on horseback trips.

All that is wonderful, but White Bird Hill also has a human history and is a place that has been enhanced by man. The Salmon River once carved Idaho into two pieces. The single south-north connection was U.S. Highway 95. We were the only state in the nation whose main north-south route had one-lane bridges:

Experiencing the Gem State meant stopping, waiting, and breathing carbon monoxide. After leaving Riggins, an old, narrow highway—it looked kind of like the Burma Road in World War II—snaked more than twenty-five hundred vertical feet up White Bird Hill. Heavy trucks could do maybe ten miles an hour as they belched clouds of diesel fumes. I called it the Goat Trail.

When I was first elected governor of Idaho in 1970, I pledged that something better than the Goat Trail would tie my north Idaho home to the rest of the state. A new highway was built with an easier grade and passing lanes. And the old road became one of the most moving places to learn of an epic journey in Northwest history.

The slopes of White Bird Hill were the site of a famous Nez Perce ambush after Chief Joseph and his people fled the U.S. cavalry in 1877. Outnumbered two to one, the Indians used small canyons and hillocks to deliver a classic ambush. The Nez Perce killed thirty-four soldiers at a cost of three wounded. They fled, resulting in a pursuit that would not end for nearly a thousand miles, at a barren battle site in eastern Montana just thirty miles from the Canadian border. Roughly a century later, as interior secretary, I helped find the resources to establish Nez Perce National Historical Park, with sites in four states, to mark a chapter in the opening of the West and the suppression of aboriginal peoples that must never be forgotten.

The old road up White Bird Hill is used for car and walking tours of its namesake battle. With whistling winds, hawks soaring overhead in air currents, and deer bounding out of the bushes, the hill is a place where you not only learn but somehow feel what happened on a June morning more than 120 years ago.

The top of White Bird Hill has a view south to 9,377-foot He Devil Mountain, the highest peak of a range that helps form the deepest canyon in North America. The Seven Devils Range divides the Snake River from the Salmon, its principal tributary. The elevation of the Snake River as it flows through Hells Canyon, and forms the border between Idaho and Oregon, is twelve hundred feet above sea level. The mountains rise nearly eight thousand vertical feet on the Idaho side, and close to seven thousand feet in Oregon. Alpine flowers, lakes, and a few permanent snowfields are found in the Seven Devils. Various species of cactus, poison ivy, rattlesnakes, and black widow spiders inhabit the bottom of the canyon.

The Northwest's power utilities once dreamed and schemed to build six-hundred-foot-high dams in the canyons of the Snake and Salmon. The paint splotches marking the Nez Perce and High Mountain Sheep dam sites can still be seen by rafting parties floating down the Snake River. In the utilities' mind-set, such dams were another human enhancement. But the upper reaches of Hells Canyon had already been dammed three times. The remaining hundred miles of canyon, I felt, were best kept wild. Salmon could spawn, bighorn sheep could balance on cliff faces, and two-footed creatures could feel the waves of Wild Sheep Rapids.

I fought to create a Hells Canyon National Recreation Area that would leave the remainder of the Snake River undammed and a River of No Return Wilderness that would assure that nobody would ever plug the Salmon River with concrete.

"A Victory for Selfishness," headlined an editorial in the pro-dam *Wenatchee (Wash.) World* newspaper when the national recreation area was approved by Congress in 1975. How small-minded that prose looks two decades later. Thousands of people visit the canyon in jet boats or on float trips every year. The middle fork of the Salmon River is recognized as one of the world's great whitewater rafting locations. Tourism, almost all of it outdoors-related, has become a $1.5 billion piece of the Idaho economy.

It is, too, at White Bird Hill that I can get steamed up over my greatest frustration in politics. The Salmon River gets its name from the hundreds of thousands of fish that once spawned in its pools, eddies, and side streams. Meriwether Lewis was fed one of them by friendly Indians after staggering over the Continental Divide at Lemhi Pass into the valley of the upper Salmon.

In the mid-1950s, about four hundred thousand salmon returned up the Snake River system each year, most heading for such unspoiled tributaries as the Salmon, Clearwater, and Imnaha Rivers. I would picnic with my young family at Bruce's Eddy on the Clearwater and wade into the river with hopes of hooking a chinook salmon or steelhead, the Northwest's fighting and famously tasty species of seagoing trout.

No more. The fish are disappearing from the river system. Idaho did not have a sportfishing season for salmon from 1979 to 1997. Snake River salmon runs are on the endangered species list. People mount candlelight vigils at the weir near Redfish Lake in Idaho's Sawtooth Mountains, waiting for salmon where an average of four sockeye have returned annually in recent years. Four thousand fish once spawned there. Steelhead are still present, but in slow decline.

The reason for this loss of fish and heritage is that the Army Corps of Engineers built eight dams downstream on the Snake and Columbia Rivers. During spring runoff, young salmon were once carried down a free-flowing river system in seven to thirteen days. Now, in slack water from Lewiston, Idaho, all the way down to Bonneville Dam east of Portland, it takes forty days—with enormous mortality at each dam.

It has been nineteen years since I stood, as interior secretary, in the visitors center at Lower Granite Dam and heard colonels from the Corps of Engineers explain a Rube Goldberg-style plan for catching young salmon above the dam and then trucking and barging the smolts hundreds of miles downstream. They were sure barging would work. I wasn't. It hasn't.

I spent my last eight years as governor of Idaho trying to get the rulers of the Columbia River—the Corps and the Bonneville Power Administration—to lower reservoir levels for a couple of months in the spring to re-create a river flow that would assure the survival of salmon. They resisted, steadfast in the private anticipation—I am convinced—that salmon will disappear from the Snake and Salmon Rivers. The problem on the river will be rendered extinct.

Recently, I drove past a riffle near the Orofino airport, the spot where I caught my last salmon. I passed 717-foot-high Dworshak Dam, which inundated fifty-four miles of spawning habitat and wiped out some of the finest cutthroat trout fishing in the world. It gets me steamed up—to think of the stubborn river managers in Portland and how we failed to find a strategy that might have moved the bureaucrats.

Enough fulminating! White Bird Hill should soothe the spirit. I've had, on the whole, a happy and rewarding career as an elected official and cabinet honcho. Carol and I succeeded in prying open the space and time for a happy family life amidst all the public responsibilities. Between stints in public office, I had six years of private life to recharge my batteries. When I retired, in January 1995, it had been twenty-eight years since I lost an election.

I served in office as the West's way of life was changing. The region was no longer living off the land. Technology was supplanting traditional resource industries as the driving force of the economy. With the fall of the Soviet Union, the Pacific Northwest could now be home to the one empire still bent on world dominion—Microsoft.

A British Columbia cabinet minister of the 1960s, "Flying Phil" Gaglardi—he was famous for fast driving and speeding tickets—once exclaimed that God didn't put down forests to worship, but for man to cut down. Increasingly, however, people of the West want their natural heritage conserved and protected. They aren't machine-wrecking Luddites; in fact, many are part of a global, computer-driven information economy. They can, however, see value in an undammed river, in the golden eagles that circle far overhead, and in the opportunities that natural habitats afford humans for recreation and renewal.

Is this a change of values? In some degree, yes. I believe, however, that much of the yearning for an unspoiled West is very traditional. Fishing with my father was a treasured part of my childhood. It ought to be an experience that my grandchildren and their children can enjoy. Nowadays, people take cell phones into the backcountry, never completely freeing themselves of their everyday lives. Still, I like to think that places like Hells Canyon or the middle fork of the Salmon River provide respite from a culture in which everyone seems to be working longer and harder.

I've spent years trying to set to rest the old, usually manufactured conflicts of jobs versus the environment. In the new economy, each needs the other. Less than a decade ago, *Newsweek* magazine ran an article sneeringly titled "Appalachia West," about the decline of mining and logging in such states as Montana and Idaho. These states are now leading the nation in per capita job creation, largely because they are such attractive places to live.

The story of my life in politics won't read like a civics textbook. How could it, coming from a politician whose favorite word was *hornswoggling*?

Hornswoggling? The dictionary likens it to bamboozling, but the word carries much more for me. It means getting down and dirty with state legislators over money needed to upgrade education and get us ready to compete in the new economy. It refers to enduring feuds with Boise Cascade, a hidebound timber company that had its hide tanned in wilderness battles.

Hornswoggling is what Jimmy Carter did in his courageous decision to use presidential authority to create fifty-six million acres of national monuments in Alaska, after Cro-Magnon politicians held up national park legislation. It is what I was doing in signing off on protection of California rivers on the evening before Ronald Reagan was sworn in as president and James Watt arrived to take over the Interior Department.

I hope to pass on a bit of the joys of hornswoggling, and I fully expect others to master this art and use it to preserve, protect, and defend the American West. I'm also hoping this book lures a few more visitors to White Bird Hill.

Chapter 1

A Political
Accident

I AM A POLITICAL ACCIDENT BUT, IN 20-20 hindsight, an accident that was waiting to happen. By the end of a public career, especially one that went on for a third of a century, somebody in my shoes has a well-honed series of stories about getting into the game. My favorite story is about how my political career began without me, over drinks at the Veterans of Foreign Wars post in Orofino. I was commander of the post, which was a social watering hole, place to dance, and all-around Saturday night destination in the Clearwater Valley.

A bunch of friends were grousing about lack of money for schools and about a veteran state senator, Leonard Cardiff, who didn't seem to know it was time to hang it up.

After a few pops, my friend Bill Harris, a World War I veteran, came up with a great idea: "Hey, we'll run Cece for the legislature."

I learned of Harris's great notion when arriving a little later, and I delivered a predictable reaction: "Are you out of your mind?"

Maybe I meant it, maybe I didn't. While I did stuff in the community, legislative chambers were not part of my background. I was a lunch-bucket guy. I worked in the woods and sawmills and had never even taken a speech class during my one year at Oregon State University. I hadn't even seen the state capitol in distant Boise. My political involvement was limited to serving as Democratic committeeman for Precinct No. 4.

I put the matter out of my mind until a few days later in the local hardware store, where the owner, Bob Oud, Republican chairman in Clearwater County, decided to shoot his mouth off.

"Hey Cece," he exclaimed, "I understand they wanted you to run for the legislature and you told them no."

I replied evenly, "That's right."

"Well," he said, "it's a good thing. We'd have just beat the hell out of you."

What kind of crap is this, I asked myself. I was tired, I was dirty, but I was good and riled. I drove down to the courthouse, walked into the county treasurer's office, and asked, "Where's one of those pieces of paper you fill out if you're going to run for the legislature?"

She looked at me, pointed to the clerk's office, and said, "Across the hall, Cece." I walked over and grabbed a petition.

So much for the storytelling. The real impetus for my running was that our oldest daughter, Tana, was just starting out in elementary school. Carol and I were not happy with the school system she was entering. Idaho had no kindergartens in those days, and we had to set one up privately in the VFW hall. Property taxes didn't provide enough money. Much of our county was national forest land. And the state's education funding formula shortchanged rural schools.

Some young parents had taken concerns for their children's education to our sixty-six-year-old state senator, who replied, "Listen. That school system was good enough for me. It's good enough for them."

To the ears of a twenty-eight-year-old, those were fighting words. By the late 1950s, I and a lot of other veterans of the Korean War or World War II were feeling our oats and weren't of a mind to lower our expectations. We wanted a better world, including our little part of it. Some of us had been to the far corners of the globe, and we wanted to expand the horizons of our kids. We chafed at what had been perfectly satisfactory in the pre–World War I universe of Leonard Cardiff.

In Orofino, with a few exceptions, eighteen-year-olds were not expected to go to college. It was considered a luxury. The boys were supposed to go to work in the woods, mills, or perhaps the local mental hospital. The girls would get married young. By 1960, however, some of the younger parents wanted their kids' education to go on beyond their hometown high school. I expected my daughters to at least try college. Whatever they did, inside or outside the ivy walls, I wanted my children to have a better shot than I had.

I had a quietly galvanizing experience not long before my name was put in nomination by Bill Harris. I drove down the valley to Lewiston where Senator John F. Kennedy, campaigning for president, was to speak. The Nez Perce Indians gave Kennedy a beautiful handmade red blanket. There were a lot of introductions. But then the audience settled into quiet listening, for the man had something to say. With his distinctive references to "vigah," Kennedy promised a new energy and sense of direction to a country grown contented during the good gray Eisenhower years. He connected with me, and I went home thinking that if a forty-two-year-old guy can be president, maybe a twenty-eight-year-old lumberjack can serve in the legislature.

I also felt a sense of duty, of obligation as a citizen that went beyond a stint in the Navy. Will Rogers once quipped of these United States, "It's a great country, but you can't live in it for nothing." John F. Kennedy made a person seriously ponder the words that Rogers spoke in jest.

If I had gone out to campaign in Clearwater County declaring that the torch had been passed to a new generation of Americans, friends would have bundled me off to the state hospital that was conveniently close by. Instead, I simply found a copy of an old AFL-CIO handbook on political campaigning. It said to get a map, block it out, and try to campaign in every borough. This was back in the days before campaign consultants, attack mailings, and push polling, in which people are called and told nasty things about candidates.

Winning a state senate seat cost me a grand total of eleven dollars. I went to a local photo shop, which charged about six to take my picture, and then took it over to the *Clearwater Tribune*, which printed up five hundred business cards. I spent weekends and evenings knocking on doors and passing out my cards. One hard-to-reach constituency was a remote logging camp called Headquarters. Since I was a licensed pilot, I made a low pass over Headquarters one day and heaved a bundle of cards out the window.

It didn't seem like such an intimidating campaign to me, but apparently it was enough for Leonard Cardiff. He had retired at the start of the campaign and tried to anoint a successor.

What have I done, I asked myself when I heard the election result. It was a bit like that scene at the end of *The Candidate*, in which Robert Redford as a newly elected U.S. senator turns to his campaign manager and asks, "What do I do now?" At twenty-nine, I had just become the youngest person yet elected to the Idaho Senate. I didn't know where the little boys' room was in the state capitol, let alone the address of the Lamppost Bar, where many of the legislature's deals were cut. Even the climate would be foreign. Orofino is in the heart of forested, river-rich northern Idaho. Boise is in the arid Snake River Basin.

During sessions, Carol and I had to relocate our growing family to a small apartment in Boise. The legislature convened for sixty days every other year (until 1969, when an annual session was approved). We were paid ten dollars a day in salary plus a fifteen-dollar daily expense allowance, which ended promptly after two months. If legislators dawdled, we did it on our own ticket.

MEANWHILE, I HAD ELECTION PROMISES TO KEEP. I quickly learned that when you're a newcomer trying to shake up statehouse politics, you make three kinds of human connections—allies with common interests, lifelong friends, and lifelong enemies.

One of my first tasks was to revise a school aid formula in

which per-pupil dollars were allocated on a basis of average daily attendance in a school system. It worked to the advantage of cities, where a single junior high or high school might enroll as many as a thousand kids. Shortchanged were rural areas and little towns, which had to maintain many school buildings with smaller enrollments.

We also faced the question of whether to pay schoolteachers a living wage. In those times, the early 1960s, most teachers were women. They received a four-figure salary that was usually a family's second income. While I can think of few jobs more essential to society's well-being, teaching was not recognized then as a full-time profession.

The first tactical ally I made was a legislator from Pocatello named Perry Swisher, who had chaired the revenue committee in the house of representatives and would come over to the state senate in 1963. I was a Democrat from the north woods. He was a Republican from the plains of the Snake River. In those days before the U.S. Supreme Court's one-man, one-vote ruling, he represented about sixty thousand people. I spoke for, at most, ten thousand constituents.

But despite these differences, we shared common interests. Pocatello was an old railroad town, home to the few Democrats who could be found in eastern Idaho. Like Orofino, it had trouble paying for its schools. No local taxes came from the area's chemical plants, which were not only outside town but over the county line. Idaho State University was nontaxable.

Swisher and I began by rewriting the formula for state aid to education. We distributed dollars according to the number of classrooms, not the number of children. We included a sparcity factor to help rural schools. We fought to increase overall spending on schools so the new formula would result in more dollars going to Orofino and Pocatello.

The going wasn't easy. Redistributing the money didn't solve the problem that there wasn't enough money. If we really wanted to pay teachers a decent wage, we would have to find a source of dollars to do it. The obvious answer was to create a state sales tax.

It was on this issue that I was to acquire both a lasting friend and a relentless adversary.

Eddie Williams, a fellow legislator, was a schoolteacher and coach at Lewiston High School, one of the few men then in the teaching profession. In the legislature, Eddie became somebody I would trust with my life—and did trust with my political life. He was the best possible guy to have in a fight for better schools, or in a fight in an alley. He knew education but was your typical friendly jock. He was also tough as nails.

A veteran capital lobbyist named Tom Boise became my adversary. He was the closest there was to a Democratic Party boss in north Idaho. A small gentleman, nicely dressed and soft-spoken, he reminded me of the veteran senator played by Claude Rains in *Mr. Smith Goes to Washington*. He somehow conveyed a sense of authority in his compactness.

Tom Boise was always there, doing favors for people and finding dollars for their campaigns. He rented a suite at the Boise Hotel from which he sallied forth on behalf of clients. The man's tactic was simple: He would go back to the people he had helped, and call in the chits.

Our first run-in occurred over (of all subjects) the trading stamps that many merchants gave to their customers. The more you spent, the more stamps you got. You could trade them for merchandise at special redemption centers. A bill came before the legislature to outlaw the stamps, the idea being that store operators could then reduce prices and pass on savings to their customers. Boise was hired by the stamp people to scuttle the proposal. He paid me a visit.

"Tom, I'm going to vote for the bill," I told him. He politely urged me to reconsider. I just as politely declined.

Boise did not bluster. He just remembered, and he was meaner than hell when he did not get his way. By crossing him, you guaranteed yourself the kind of problems that politicians squirm to avoid. One of Boise's allies might vote to keep your bill bottled up in committee. Or a primary election opponent would appear. Going against Boise required that you keep a watchful eye on your flanks at all times.

The real cleavage came over a state sales tax, to which Tom Boise was adamantly opposed. He had been able to count on a solid front of Democrats from northern Idaho to vote against it. I breached that front. In 1965, a 3 percent sales tax plan passed the state house of representatives but stalled in the upper chamber. Perry Swisher, the bill's floor sponsor in the senate, raised a question that had to be answered: How could you say you were for better schools when you weren't willing to pay for them?

I was the first Democratic senator to vote for the sales tax. It passed and was signed into law by Governor Robert Smylie. Opponents forced a referendum onto the 1966 ballot.

I expected an immediate, angry reaction to the sales tax vote. Upon my return to Orofino, I scheduled a public meeting, privately anticipating a local version of a famous confrontation recounted in John F. Kennedy's book *Profiles in Courage*. In 1916, Nebraska Senator George Norris found himself vilified for voting against a bill to arm U.S. merchant ships, just before America's entry into World War I. Norris returned to Lincoln, mounted a stage before three thousand silent people, and declared: "I have come home to tell you the truth."

The public meeting in Orofino attracted a crowd of eleven people, four of them from my own family. From the lack of attendance, I concluded that people wanted good schools and were willing to pay for them, and I wasn't going to get hurt by voting for a tax that made it possible.

I hadn't factored in Tom Boise. Boise was never one to get

mad when there was the opportunity to get even. I had decided to run for governor in 1966. Tom helped persuade a conservative Salmon, Idaho, attorney named Charles Herndon to run against me in the Democratic primary. Boise put his every resource behind Herndon, who narrowly defeated me. In mid-September, however, Herndon was killed in a plane crash. The Democratic state committee was to pick his replacement as gubernatorial nominee. Tom Boise would not relent and let me have the nomination. He put up another candidate, Max Hanson, who was state director of the Farmers Home Administration. Assured by Boise that he had the votes to win, Max went out the night before the vote and mailed in his resignation from the FHA. Surprise! I eked out an 84-82 victory in the committee vote thanks in no small part to Frank Church's aide, Verda Barnes, who stayed up all night working the phones for me.

As Eddie Williams muttered after this latest face-off with Boise, "We'll damned well outlive him." We did, as a matter of fact. Boise suffered a stroke and died soon after the state Democratic convention.

The year 1966 was the only time I ever lost a public election—and I managed to lose both the gubernatorial primary and the general. The subsequent death of primary winner Charles Herndon had kept me in contention, but I would get no second chance in the general election. The contest was a strange four-way affair. An ultraconservative state senator named Don Samuelson upset Governor Smylie in the Republican primary as the incumbent tried for a fourth term. Samuelson was a sales tax opponent, which prompted Perry Swisher to jump into the race as an independent on a platform supporting the tax. A Lewiston businessman, Phil Jungert, ran on a pro-gambling platform.

When it was all sorted out, Samuelson had beaten me by ten thousand votes. The sales tax, however, won approval by the largest margin of victory of any candidate or referendum in state history.

The defeat was hard to take, and there were recriminations. Some claimed that Perry Swisher drained away support that would have given me victory. Swisher retorted that his voters would have gone to Samuelson and given him a much more decisive victory. We were to grumble at each other for quite some time.

Thirty years later, with four wins under my belt, I don't mind recalling what the late Chicago Mayor Richard Daley said when blamed for Hubert Humphrey's narrow defeat in the 1968 presidential race: "He lost because he didn't get enough votes."

BY THE END OF MY 1966 RACE, CAROL WANTED NO MORE part of campaigning, and I told her that I was through with politics. I think it was the first lie of our marriage. We moved to Lewiston and I went into the insurance business. Two years later, I was back in the state senate.

Why return? Well, for starters, it was a nice place to work. Legislatures were pleasant and collegial places in those days long before the advent of nonstop campaigning, so-called wedge issues, and the take-no-prisoners partisanship symbolized by the Newt Gingriches of the world. We may have disagreed along philosophical lines, but we disagreed without bitterness, rancor, or threats of revenge in the next election. We weren't nasty to each other.

Of course, there was horsetrading. Certain corporations acted like lords of the legislature. It's a particular trait of utilities. The Idaho Power Company assumed it owned the Republicans in the Idaho Legislature, just as the Washington Water Power Company threw its weight (and cash) around in Olympia and the Pacific Power and Light Company of Oregon asserted itself in Salem.

At times, legislators would indulge in gamesmanship,

drafting a bill adverse to the interests of Idaho Power or Boise Cascade or Potlatch, the state's biggest timber companies. One senior colleague, Pop Murphy, used to call it whiskey-and-steak legislating. For example, a bill would be introduced to increase the assessed valuation of Idaho Power property. One famous "steak generator" was a bill to increase the per-ton tax on truckers.

Company lobbyists would immediately host dinners to let legislators hear arguments against the bill. The lawmakers would listen, eat a good meal, see the light—even with blurry vision from much bourbon—and the proposed rate-relief measure or tax on timber inventory would disappear from the agenda.

The governor's office had little influence over legislating or, it seemed, over the state. Don Samuelson tried to govern Idaho with a foot planted firmly in his mouth. Every day I became more anxious for a rematch. The incumbent was malaprop-prone, vulnerable on old issues like education, and especially tone deaf to a new movement that came of age in 1970 and has stayed center stage ever since. That movement's cause was conservation of the environment.

I was still worried about schools, but my reason for concern had shifted. Basic education had improved, but the best and brightest high school graduates still felt they had to go out of state to find a quality college education. And after college, they wouldn't come back to Idaho, because there weren't enough opportunities to draw them back. If they wanted to make a living using brain rather than brawn, they had to go someplace else.

The environment issue was championed by friends with whom I had hunted and fished. Beginning in 1962, a handful of Idaho's environmental activists took a five-day fishing trip each May, usually to Owyhee Reservoir in the high desert. They plotted how to keep more dams out of Hells Canyon. They sought ways to bring state issues to national attention. It was a coup when *Life* magazine ran a photo spread that brought word of the proposed

open-pit molybdenum mine in the White Cloud Mountains to
the newsstands of America. The battle over the White Clouds
would help make me the first Western governor elected on an
environmental platform.

RUNNING FOR GOVERNOR WAS STILL AN INFORMAL
affair, and the 1970 campaign had a hand-to-mouth flavor. I
drove around the state in a white Chevy Impala, usually in the
company of a young Lewiston TV reporter named John Hough,
who signed on as press secretary after three other fellows turned
down the job. Governor Samuelson faced few logistical difficulties and moved at a more rapid clip courtesy of the private plane
of potato magnate J. R. "Jack" Simplot.

We had to remember to stash away our smokes when campaigning in Mormon towns in eastern Idaho. Staying at the house
of a local bishop, we could not break out the Cutty Sark for a
nightcap. One night in Rigby, Hough and I discovered we had
just ten dollars between the two of us. We were hungry, we had
to buy gas to get out of town, and we needed a place to spend the
night. A meal took half the money. I had a notion that the owner
of the local Husky service station, an active Democrat, would
donate a tank of gas to the campaign. Hough pumped $5.50
worth of gas—enough to fill the tank in those days—and proudly
told the station owner we were in town. "I'd like to make a donation," he replied. "Take fifty cents off the bill." We were flat
broke, but I phoned headquarters and found a supporter in Idaho
Falls who would put us up for the night.

Campaigning in the Chevy paid off. I won, besting Samuelson
by a margin of just under eleven thousand votes. I carried only
thirteen of Idaho's forty-four counties, but won the places where a
majority of voters lived.

That first victory in 1970 was the grandest, and instilled in me a sense of limitless possibilities for the state I loved. While never approaching the prose of John Kennedy or his writer Ted Sorenson, I delivered an inaugural address pledging "a new beginning." We would pursue what I called a "quest for greatness" by protecting Idaho's grand natural beauty and responding to an overwhelming public desire for top-notch public schools.

It was Theodore Roosevelt, my kind of Republican, who said, "The government is us. We are the government, you and I." Being governor gave me a chance to feel those words. Of course, I couldn't order things to happen. Statehouse governing is a process of making good appointments, negotiating compromises—sometimes settling for less than a full loaf—and picking times when you mount the bully pulpit.

A DECADE IN THE LEGISLATURE HAD TAUGHT ME valuable lessons in how to advance my agenda. The first lesson: Keep pluggin' away. It can take eons to pass reforms in a conservative state. It was 1955 when Governor Smylie first asked the legislature to lower the voting age to nineteen. It finally happened on my watch, sixteen years later. In 1971, we still didn't have public kindergartens, the cause that had first drawn me to politics more than a decade earlier. I proposed a statewide, state-funded system of kindergartens to the legislature in 1971, and again in 1972, 1973, and 1974, before they were at last approved in 1975.

Some people thought kindergartens were a communist plot, the state's way of beginning indoctrination at the earliest possible age. We've always had an unhealthy supply of right-wing kooks in Idaho, and in their minds this issue was up there with water fluoridation. We also came up against the argument from some overprotective parents that kids were being taken out of the home too early.

The legislature ultimately chose to fund kindergartens, while making attendance voluntary. The kindergartens were an instant hit. And nobody ever uncovered evidence of Reds under anybody's bed.

At the same time I kept hammering on the Republican-controlled chambers to allocate more money to schools. They responded much too slowly to my way of thinking. But even if it was glacial, there was movement.

I had to believe, or I would have left politics in the 1960s, that patience would have its rewards. Without patience, talented people get flummoxed by politics. They stalk away without seeing the benefits of quiet work and step-by-step progress. Or they become militant, choosing to lie down in front of a logger's bulldozer rather than spend the hours upon hours needed to negotiate a land use plan that protects streambeds and spawning salmon.

THE SECOND LESSON I HAD LEARNED IN MY LAWMAKING days, a product of legislative poker playing, was to always act as if I held a strong hand. This tactic was particularly valuable when, as governor, I had to deal with that toughest species of poker player, the self-made entrepreneur.

I set out in the early 1970s to get Idaho a stream protection law and to stop use of the Snake River as an open sewer. We had twenty-three industrial plants and two municipalities dumping untreated wastes directly into the river. Jack Simplot had the biggest processing plant, at Heyburn, Idaho, which was unloading everything, up to and including the potato peelings, out the discharge pipes. He was also the state's most powerful businessman, the nut I had to crack to make a go of any cleanup.

When we met I looked Simplot in the eye and told him that he was going to have to install secondary treatment at the facilities where he processed his spuds. "You will do this or I will wait for low water, when the outflow pipes are exposed, and take a TV crew down there and personally put plugs in those pipes," I threatened.

Simplot was blunt in return, saying words to this effect: "Jesus Christ, governor, one of the reasons I built that plant on the banks of the river was so that I would have somewhere to dump my trash."

"That was when your plant was the only plant and the river could handle it," I replied.

We went to the mat for a time, and then he put an offer on the table. "If you make me do it," he said, "will you give me your word that you will make all my competitors do as I do?"

We shook on it. He kept his word. I kept mine. I didn't make him a high-profile target, and he was the first to build a secondary treatment plant. Simplot called me up one afternoon with an unusually worded invitation to the dedication: "Why don't we go out and start up that turd crusher you made me build?" We flew up the Snake River to Heyburn in the plane that had carried my former opponent Don Samuelson across the state. Jack was expansive as he pointed out his holdings. The holdings, too, were expansive.

Simplot had the last laugh. In order to keep potato peelings out of the river, he built a low-pressure pipeline that was connected to a feedlot, where his cattle were fed a diet of spud leftovers. While improving the Snake River, he made even more money.

We took the first big step toward a technology economy during my first years as governor. Hewlett-Packard was pondering whether to put a plant in Boise or pick a site in Medford, Oregon. I had David Packard visit my office. He was a remarkable guy, a computer entrepreneur, Silicon Valley pioneer, deputy defense sec-retary—and somebody who spent years trying to persuade Cali-fornia's Republican Party to put up competent moderate candidates instead of right-wing ideologues.

While no one had made this discovery yet, went my spiel, Idaho was an excellent place to make computers. We had low taxes, and we had a workforce with many people who were first-generation off the farm. They were willing to deliver a full day's work for a day's pay.

Packard listened politely and then asked in a level voice: "What type of tax concessions is the state willing to give?" He was obviously alluding to inducements offered by Oregon.

I took a deep breath and set out to sell him on a difficult argument. "We don't believe in existing businesses subsidizing new businesses," I told him. "When you come to Idaho you become a citizen, and we all play by the same rules. A few years down the line and you'll be an old-timer. Do you want to subsi-dize the next guy who comes along?"

It was a nervous moment. After a brief pause, Packard grunted: "Makes sense. That's the way to go." He moved on to other questions. We captured the computer plant and gained a top-notch corporate citizen. Hewlett-Packard put up front-end money on a sewage treatment plant, practiced recycling, and was an innovator in heavy metals extraction.

THE FINAL LESSON, WHICH I HAD BEGUN TO GRASP AS A legislator, was not fully learned until one of the major crises of my first tenure as governor. There are bound to be some dis-tressing events, and my first was the 1976 Teton Dam collapse: What happened on that June morning took eleven lives and cost $2 billion.

In every governor's administration, there are projects on which you get endless assurances from federal and state agencies as well as from promoters. Still, you have a funny feeling in your gut. Trust your gut! Seek a second or third opinion—above all, an independent opinion—to check out gut-level concerns.

Teton Dam, a 305-foot-high Bureau of Reclamation project in eastern Idaho, was supposedly fail-safe. But it set loose the biggest flood seen in the Northwest since the retreat of Pleistocene glaciers unleashed trapped waters of Lake Missoula more than ten thousand years ago.

"I was not a supporter of Teton Dam," I tell the curious. "It was an unnecessary structure built for a few irrigators."

A few astute interrogators have come at me with an uncomfortable follow-up question: Had I actively opposed Teton Dam, which was built on my watch as governor?

I respond with careful candor: "Originally yes, but then I acquiesced to it."

I had doubts about Teton Dam. I wondered just how many irrigators would benefit, and whether they could just as well tap into groundwater and leave the Teton River valley alone. My staff was split. My first chief of staff, Eddie Williams, was in favor of the dam. Several of my younger advisers were against it.

But there were, as they say, countervailing forces. The dam enjoyed fervent support from irrigators in eastern Idaho as well as from its prospective builder, the U.S. Bureau of Reclamation. Irrigated agriculture was central to the state's economy. The Idaho congressional delegation lined up behind the dam, from respected Democratic Senator Frank Church, an early conservationist, to respected GOP Senator Len Jordan. I was working with these guys on issues like the birds of prey sanctuary and the Sawtooth National Recreation Area. I needed them.

It is likely this turkey of a project would have taken flight even if I had tried to shoot it down. At least I tell myself that.

Candidly, however, I must admit that a variety of delay tactics can be deployed once a governor decides to oppose a project. A chief executive can often force bureaucracies to seriously weigh dissenting opinions and give grudging consideration to alternatives.

I don't look back once a decision is made—never have. In this case, perhaps, I should have looked more closely. At Teton Dam, problems were unfolding while responsible parties dropped into a bureaucracy's secretive, defensive crouch.

A parallel situation emerged in Washington state. Governor Dan Evans was somewhat skeptical when the Washington Public Power Supply System (WPPSS, pronounced "Whoops") set out to build five nuclear power plants. He was told, however, that a power-hungry Northwest would suffer brownouts if the massive construction project were not undertaken at once. The Bonneville Power Administration ridiculed studies that questioned power use projections and suggested conservation as an alternative. Evans acquiesced, despite private worries about whether WPPSS could manage a project of such magnitude. The eventual consequence was four abandoned, partially built reactors and the biggest bond default in American history. (A few years later, as chairman of the Northwest Power Planning Council, Evans helped block private utilities' planned nuclear projects, possibly preventing a second financial meltdown.)

Doubters were dismissed in Idaho as construction started on Teton Dam. The U.S. Geological Survey, somewhat timidly, questioned site stability and the ash flows and volcanic rock to which the earthen dam was anchored. The critical assessments were buried in the Bureau of Reclamation's Denver office. Like WPPSS, BuRec had institutional pride and an ideological commitment at stake. The agency even managed to ignore a warning from its own project manager of "unusually large" fissures in rock formations of the right canyon wall.

I should have had my political antennae out and picked up the voices of caution. Surely I wasn't going to hear warnings from the Bureau of Reclamation. The people who tentatively, sometimes obliquely, raised concerns about site stability should have felt comfortable bringing their doubts straight to the governor's office.

On Thursday, June 3, 1976, leaks were noticed in the newly completed dam. By Friday, water was coming out in three places. On Saturday morning, engineers spotted a muddy creek flowing out of the right abutment adjacent to the dam. Only then did BuRec engineers at the site inform their higher-ups. State government was not informed. The reservoir spilled out toward the Mormon farming towns of the valley below.

It's strange to say about a disaster that took eleven lives, but we were incredibly lucky. If the dam had broken a few hours earlier, in the night, thousands of lives would have been lost in the towns of Sugar City and Rexburg. People were warned just in time to reach higher ground before a wall of mud and water hit their homes. Downstream, below where the Teton River joins the Snake River, the town of Idaho Falls would not have had the time to mobilize thousands of volunteers to sandbag levees along the river.

Above all, the organizational structure of the Mormon Church worked with a speed and efficiency that emergency management agencies still study. The church's Relief Society was instantly on the scene to aid those who had made it to higher ground but had to watch as their possessions were swept away or were burned when a gasoline storage tank was ruptured by logs in Rexburg. Later, I stood with church president Spencer Kimball in the gym at Ricks College, giving assurances that their way of life would be restored.

The Bureau of Reclamation was curiously unapologetic. After the disaster, political cartoonist Pat Oliphant accurately captured the agency's attitude. He depicted a beefy BuRec bureaucrat sitting at his desk and declaring, "If we listened to every environmentalist dingbat, we'd never get anything built." In the background Teton Dam was bursting, with cows and houses hurtling into the air.

Nobody can ever unscramble an egg, but I was to influence the subsequent course of events. I became interior secretary three months after the Teton Dam disaster. The Bureau of Reclamation was, by then, trying to wash its hands of responsibility, hinting at deficiencies in the contractor's work on the dam. Floating a trial balloon, the Interior Department solicitor general suggested that we sue the contractor. One of my aides replied that the first witness for the builder, Morrison-Knudsen, would be Cecil Andrus.

The contractor had followed the Bureau of Reclamation's recommendations. I knew it. The dam's failure was due to a design flaw caused by BuRec engineers in the Denver office. I insisted that blame go where it belonged. The federal government was forced to pay all the claims. The chief engineer in Denver decided to take early retirement: He sat at the desk where the buck stopped.

A wiser man, I returned to the governor's office for the second time in 1987. Incredibly, some irrigators were agitating to have Teton Dam rebuilt. An unrepentant Bureau of Reclamation was declaring its willingness to undertake the project if people wanted it. I listened to my gut, kept my counsel, and erected a wall of conditions—broad public support, fish and wildlife protection, a favorable cost-benefit analysis done by an unbiased source—around proposals to bring Teton Dam back from the dead.

"When they solve all that, they can come to me," I announced.

And you know, they never did.

Chapter 2

GOVERNING LIKE A NORMAL GUY

A N ABC-TV CREW FLEW INTO BOISE in 1993 with the assignment to film Idaho's governor doing normal, mundane things. The crew's journey was occasioned by the search for a governor who behaved like a normal citizen. My daily routines became fodder for a weekly TV newsmagazine.

The lenses of network news pointed at me as I cooked breakfast in my own home. The camera followed me as I slipped behind the wheel of my own car and drove to work. The people from ABC collected footage of a governor walking unescorted into his office, and lugging an overnight bag into the coach section of an airplane. I was captured in the act of mowing the lawn in front of my house, a task often performed by convicts in front of a state-owned mansion in other capitals.

Ordinary activities for most Americans, but not for most American governors. I tuned in to *PrimeTime Live* to watch myself act like an everyday citizen, but ended up staring in fascination as the show nailed my colleagues. Viewers were treated to a parade of limousines, state airplanes, and state troopers acting as servants. Governor Doug Wilder of Virginia ducked an ambush interview with Sam Donaldson, who wanted to know something about his use of helicopters. Governor Bruce King of New Mexico, who did submit to questions, groped for words to explain what he did with his generous entertainment budget.

The perks were one of the first things Carol and I noticed after my initial gubernatorial victory in 1970. Taken aback at the cocoon of security and staff we witnessed elsewhere, my wife turned to me at one point and said, "Idaho is just a different state."

My home number was, for a time, still listed in the phone book. Of course, my wife and I did get a message from a man who called to say, "This is Peppy. Tell the governor that Peppy is going to kill him." Such messages were, fortunately, infrequent. I did in fact hear more from Peppy, who came to my office on some unfathomable mission. He beat the glass out of the front doors to the state capitol to gain entry. The doors were unlocked at the time.

Still, Idaho was a place of informality and trust, where people expected to buttonhole the governor and not be intercepted on the way. At home the governor remained in charge of fixing his kids' bicycles. The family let him know, in Carol's words, "the instant he got too big for his britches."

As governor for fourteen years—1971 to 1977, and again 1987 to 1995—I watched my counterparts get bigger and bigger britches. It was at first amusing, but then increasingly discomforting, to observe the retinues and limousines and residences that made easy and isolated the lives of many cohorts.

In American government, these governors were elected representatives of the people. But no effort was spared to keep them separate and aloof from the people. The apartness was more than physical. It seemed to me that our country's governing class was losing touch because it did not share the everyday headaches of the governed.

A decaying highway infrastructure cannot be appreciated when you are traveling by helicopter, or talking on the phone in the back of a limousine. Overcrowded airports are never a problem when you get driven to a private hangar and whisked aboard your own plane. A cook in the governor's mansion means you have to learn food prices only when ambush interviews threaten at election time. An omnipresent legal adviser spares you from deciphering regulations that you promulgate. A doting personal staff means you never have to stand in line for a permit, let alone take tests for a driver's license.

I did stand in line for my driver's license. The examiner looked up, did a double take, and observed, "Oh, it's you." Only as I walked back to the car did I look at my new license and notice that, under hair color, she had written, "Glossy."

George Reedy, who was Lyndon Johnson's press secretary, once coined a phrase—"the Xanadu effect"—to characterize the isolated American politician. A friend told me that it was inspired by the first line of a poem by Coleridge, "In Xanadu did Kublai Khan a stately pleasure dome decree. . . ."

The reference, unmistakably, was to officeholders cut off from reality and inhabiting a world created by their entourages. I saw isolation show up in small ways and large whenever the nation's governors convened. It was like that in 1971 when I was a green-horn attending my first governors conference, and a quarter-century later when I was leaving office.

At one meeting, Mario Cuomo complained that his back was hurting. Behind him, a man whispered into his hand micro-phone. Another gentleman with a wire protruding from his ear instantly appeared with a piece of plywood to prop behind the governor of New York.

Illinois Governor Dan Walker, a colleague in the 1970s, would not enter a room until two security men looked under the tables and also inspected the chair in which the gubernatorial fanny was about to rest. They would stand guard at the governor's seat, whereupon Walker would make his entrance. He would later be more closely guarded. Walker was convicted of taking bribes and served a prison sentence.

We convened at Jackson Hole one year, and the daughter of the governor of Wyoming brought a welcome basket of fruit, cheeses, and a bottle of wine up to Ronald Reagan's suite. The security men snatched the wine, opened the bottle, and poured its contents into the sink.

Reagan struck me as the most isolated of governors, inhab-iting a world accessible to only his and Nancy's wealthy friends, a few old actor buddies, and the staff who choreographed his every move. He was a person who took direction well, but was at a loss without it.

An unforgettable set-to came during a National Governors' Association winter meeting at the Washington Hilton. We were seated at a round table with one microphone for every two seats. The session was drearily dull except for a picket line of welfare mothers outside the hotel. The ladies' presence had the unfortunate effect of launching the governor of California into his tales about welfare queens. Reagan was out of sorts anyway. Back home, California newspapers had disclosed the governor's use of a variety of loopholes to avoid paying state income taxes.

The security arrangements broke down and a throng of demonstrators burst into the room. A seat at the governor's table was available because Governor Forrest Anderson of Montana had picked that moment to go relieve himself. His chair didn't stay empty for long. A heavyset welfare demonstrator came up to the table, grabbed a mike, and declared that she could not afford to feed her children nutritious food.

"It doesn't look to me like you've been missing any meals," Reagan declared.

She grinned broadly, looked the Gipper in the eye, and went for the jugular: "Honey, if I had to live on the amount of taxes you pay, I'd be skinny as a rail."

I RETURNED TO THE IDAHO GOVERNOR'S OFFICE IN 1987 after a ten-year absence. Reagan had moved on to the White House. But a new generation of would-be presidents seemed to be surrounded by even more aides, political handlers, and protection. I faced a choice of going with the flow or rebelling. Since I had spent years extolling Idahoans as fiercely independent folk, I picked the latter course. I informed my predecessor's security detail that the governor's life was not in danger. They were to get back in uniform, get back out on the highways, and catch speeders.

Elaborate protection of governors is, after all, largely for show. If somebody really wants to assassinate any politician aside from the president or vice president, he or she will get the job done. A bevy of escorts slows a public figure who is passing through a crowded room, enhancing the chances of any would-be assailant.

Of course, not everybody wants to get around quickly, particularly when politicos and pundits are gathered. The personal retinue is to politicians what a harem of cows is to a bull elk. It is designed to indicate potency, attract attention, and lay down the scent of ambition.

Bill Clinton served as governor of one of America's smallest, poorest states while having the nation's biggest set of presidential dreams. He advertised that fact by arriving everywhere with an ever-trailing comet's tail of advisers, guards, and reporters. I'll give Clinton credit for a quick mind and for doing his time in the trenches working on task forces. When governors were in public session, however, he was forever leaning against the wall, entertaining admirers with stories or—endlessly—spinning the press. It produced a funny incident at the 1990 meeting of the Democratic Leadership Council in New Orleans. Clinton was in his second hour of nonstop interviews in the back of the room when Cragg Hines of the *Houston Chronicle* quipped, "Would somebody please give that guy the hook?"

In an earlier era, it was Ronald Reagan who showed the actor's knack for the attention-getting performance. Grand entrances would become a hallmark of an exquisitely stage-managed presidency. Reagan was a quick study when it came to effective delivery of his lines. When his own wits were required, however, he was "closed for repairs," in Kitty Kelley's telling phrase. The person on hand to direct the former Hollywood leading man—or, more accurately, the leading man's best friend—was future attorney general Ed Meese. He was at the time Reagan's legal adviser, and was a very smart guy. Meese would lean over and whisper in his boss's ear or put a card in front of him. Reagan would look up and speak as if the words had come that instant from his heart.

Reagan was the ultimate example of the leader enclosed by courtiers. He did not show up for meetings of governors' task forces where the real work was done. Instead, he would waltz in late in the day, corral TV cameras in the foyer, and speak in flawless sound bites.

Only once, in private, was he called to account. A panel of governors had spent two days hammering out a policy position on ways to get people off welfare. The governor of California never spent a minute with the committee. When our work was done, however, Reagan floated in, delivered his usual do-away-with-the-cheaters speech, and then huddled privately with the committee's chairman, Nelson Rockefeller. I was vice chairman, and history's witness to a memorable policy exchange between a future Republican president and a future GOP vice president.

"I cannot support this report. I will oppose it if you present it to the full meeting," Reagan declared.

"Ron, we've been working on this for two days," Rocky snapped. "Ron, if you do that, I'll take the microphone and tell the world how fucking dumb you really are."

Reagan didn't say a word when the committee report was submitted and approved the next day.

Rockefeller was the ultimate in opulent governors, with a personal fortune to support his style and underwrite his retinue.

In one foray, he traveled by private jet to the Northwest in 1972 to hold fund-raisers for Washington Governor Dan Evans. The two men were flying from Spokane to Seattle when Rockefeller voiced a desire to see the North Cascades. The governors took a twenty-minute jet joyride through remote mountain passes that Evans, a backpacker, normally slogged for days to reach. And Rockefeller wasn't about to eat the food served at the Evans' fund-raiser at the Seattle Center. A steak was specially prepared for the governor of New York by Canlis, the city's swankiest steakhouse, and rushed to the airport for consumption.

UNLIKE REAGAN, ROCKEFELLER, AND CLINTON, I never ran for the White House. I served a single four-year sentence in Washington, D.C., as President Carter's secretary of the interior. I arranged the schedule on subsequent capital trips so as to spend as few nights as possible in and around the District of Columbia.

I was born poor and instilled with the lesson that you do your own lifting. When I was a kid we carried in water for drinking, and I was eleven years old before I realized that most people went to the john indoors.

My entrance into politics was not the culmination of networking that dated back to college. I lived in Orofino, Idaho, and confined my activism to the Lutheran Church League, the local VFW post, and the PTA. One of my preparations for public office was the Fourth of July lumberjack celebration where I painted a hundred-foot-high pole in red, white, and blue.

My wife is notoriously unimpressed by status and title. Over the years my flights of ambition have invariably been greeted with the admonition, "You've got to be kidding." Carol and I went fishing shortly after my first election as governor. Not a nibble came my way. I created commotion by complaining, changing lures, and digging into my box of gear. With a take-this look in her eyes, Carol asked, "Why don't you toss your business card into the water so they know who's up here?"

The Andrus family maintained a normal life before, during, and after my time in the governor's office and the Interior Department. We built a cabin on Cascade Reservoir, about ninety miles north of Boise, and escaped there by ourselves every possible weekend. My wife and daughters were never hesitant about giving me advice around the dinner table. As my daughter Tracy puts it, "We were never a shy family." They were probably a little bit to the left of me politically, my wife being a preservationist on most environmental issues and my daughters pro-choice on abortion. No subject was taboo in our family discussions.

It helped me politically that I was just "Dad" at home, treated no differently than if I had been back at an insurance office in Lewiston or a mill in Orofino. Idaho voters would never have given four terms to a governor who put on airs. And no living creature in Idaho, be it on two legs or four, is known for obedience or passivity. I had that lesson reinforced a few years back, in my twelfth year as Idaho's chief executive, when I became the first American governor ever kicked in the face by a mule.

An elk hunt has been my annual autumn getaway. The presence of my name on the ballot never kept me out of the mountains. I've also enjoyed the challenge of trying to escape for three or four days without alerting the capital press corps. If Henry Kissinger could sneak off to China, I would pay a secret visit to the back side of the Sawtooths.

Having just acquired a mule called Ruthie, I took her along as a beast of burden to carry out the elk meat. The hunt started out a success. I shot a big bull elk, dressed him, and walked back to camp to get my meat saw so I could skin the beast and quarter him. The horse and mule, with packsaddles and meat sacks, were tied to a pine tree.

As I was about to start back up the mountain, my hunting pard'ner, Dick Meiers, arrived back at camp and suggested we take the mule and horse with us and just make one trip. We put the packsaddles on the animals, went back to the elk, tied the animals to some small pines, and went to work skinning, quartering, and sacking the elk.

As we prepared to load, Ruthie expressed a strong dislike for the smell of blood. I put a firm hand on her halter as Dick leaned down to tighten the cinch. Ruthie went ballistic. She reared up and struck me in the face with her left forefoot and then somehow nailed Dick in the forehead. I rolled down the slope until a pine tree stopped my tumbling descent.

I had a gash from the center of my forehead down to the corner of my left eye and a broken nose. I was a bloody and bleeding mess. Dick was unconscious and bleeding severely from a deep gash laterally across his forehead. While I hurt like the devil, I could still think straight, but it looked as if Dick's brains had been exposed as well as scrambled. I made a compress of my shirt to stop his bleeding and and then learned firsthand how a severe concussion inhibits intelligent conversation, behavior, and language.

When Dick regained consciousness, he didn't know who he was, where he was, or what was going on. He kept asking me over and over, "What happened?" He finally looked up and saw blood all over my face and said, "Jesus Christ, what happened to you?" "The same thing that happened to you," I replied.

While he continued to ask, "What happened," I explained that we had to get the hell out of there. I led Dick and the horse back to our camp and old Ruthie followed along behind. When we reached camp, I sat Dick on a chair and improved the compress, stripped the saddles from the animals, tied them, and gave each a bucket of water, not knowing if I would ever see them again.

I had one trapping of office with me back in the tent, a state police handheld radio. I told the police we had suffered a hunting accident and that we needed medical attention and would be at the intersection of Highway 21 and Five-Mile Creek in an hour and a half.

We went down the trail, replaying the same conversation. "What happened?" "We've got to get the hell out of here." "Jesus Christ, what happened to you?"

We made it to my pickup truck and I drove down to the intersection. Sure enough, an Emergency Medical Services van and U.S. Forest Service people were there to meet us. I was beat up, but Ruthie had done greater damage to Dick. Normally the most polite of men, he cut loose with a string of cuss words when the paramedics wouldn't let him drink anything. I hastened to make apologies to a pretty young nurse. "Governor, I've heard all those words before," she replied. "I work for the Forest Service."

"Governor Injured in Hunting Accident," read the Associated Press bulletin. My political opponents were asked to react. "Hell, when I found out he'd been kicked in the head, I knew he'd be all right," opined GOP Senator Steve Symms.

For a while, I doubted it. Ruthie had fractured my skull, broken my nose, busted bones inside my right eye, and embedded pine needles and dirt in my wounds. The attending physician warned that my eye would acquire a permanent tilt. "Doc, a little tilt to the right in Idaho is no problem," I told him.

As offers for Ruthie came pouring in—the mule had remained peacefully in camp after doing her damage—I entertained the thought that a bodyguard might have been a good idea. Nah! My busted nose and squinting eye notwithstanding, there are more gains than pains to be realized from going without an entourage.

I'VE FOUND THAT IT DOESN'T HURT TO GET INTO A COLD car. The rear end of an airplane gets to its destination at exactly the same time as the front end. Along the way, being with the governed, you learn a few things and get the chance to act on people's problems.

During my first stint as governor, in the 1970s, I had to endure lousy commercial air service out of Boise. Northwest Orient Airlines lavished attention on its international flights, while scrimping on milk runs in the Mountain West.

A governor's complaint letters get read. Even more careful attention is paid to those from a cabinet officer. I happened to be interior secretary when a major new trans-Pacific air route was up for approval. Northwest was a candidate. Using official stationery, I related to the Civil Aeronautics Board past instances of delays and stranded passengers bound for my home state. The airline was quick to fetch my letter out of CAB filings. It was one of those rare, pleasurable instances of a corporation forced into submissiveness. How, Northwest asked, could they improve service? What did airline travelers in Idaho, Montana, and North Dakota look for in an airline?

Together with aides who had suffered through Northwest's service, I put together a list of suggestions starting with on-time flights. In spite of President Carter's business in private life, I felt free to demand better food and fewer goobers. Northwest has become a much better airline in the years since my complaint.

I was eventually driven from the Boise phone book when

news of my listed number reached bars around town and I began getting late-night calls from town drunks. Before that, however, an out-of-the-blue evening phone call led to the most rewarding experience of my tenure as governor.

"My grandson is going to die," a woman's voice said over the phone. I asked her to come see me at my office the next day. Her daughter had a nine-year-old son, thin and pale, with a heart deficiency. He needed an operation and the family had no health insurance.

I knew some people at a childrens hospital in California. We got on the horn and had the boy admitted as a patient. I took Scotty and his grandmother to the airport, the boy looking very small and vulnerable in the backseat. The nurses gave me a pessimistic assessment just before his operation.

But his hospital stay was successful. Scotty survived, and I found myself on a happy drive back out to the airport to pick up the family. The little guy came off the plane with a rolled-up piece of paper. It was a child's picture of Idaho with big snowcapped mountains, an animal with a horn, and streams everywhere.

On Christmas Eve, my doorbell rang. It was Scotty, there with a plaque. Every year he came back with some small token of appreciation. I broke down that first Christmas. The trauma of the trip to the airport, and the thrill of seeing the boy OK—and looking more robust with each visit—transcended every policy initiative I had taken.

Idaho is a Republican bastion in national elections. Just once in the last forty-eight years has a Democratic presidential candidate carried the Gem State. Lyndon Johnson beat Barry Goldwater in 1964 by just five thousand votes. Nonetheless, I was able to get elected governor in 1970, 1974, 1986, and 1990. Each time, a Republican was in the White House. Were I an insulated politician, not one of these victories would have been possible.

Staying in touch is the prime prerequisite to staying alive as an Idaho Democrat. The state has elected Republicans so dumb they need to be watered, but any Democrat who hopes to stick around must have the adaptive skills of a coyote.

THERE HAVE BEEN A FEW TIMES WHEN I GOT UP ON MY high horse. Luckily, when unhorsed, I've experienced soft landings. One story deserves retelling even though it doesn't make me look too good. In it are lessons about the dangers of official arrogance.

One of my few indulgences while in Washington, D.C., was a well-known restaurant named Dominique's, about five blocks from the Interior Department. Its menu is known for such exotic fare as ostrich and rattlesnake. The owner, Dominique D'Eermo, also served as chef and informal counselor to Elizabeth Taylor for a time. After she helped husband number six, John Warner, win a Senate seat, Taylor discovered he was a workaholic who took the job seriously. The neglected Liz took solace in such Dominique's fare as chocolate truffles drowned in whipped cream and almonds.

I was dining at Dominique's one night when the proprietor came to my table with a problem. "Mr. Secretary, I seem to have run afoul of your Fish and Wildlife Service," Dominique told me. The restaurant had received a warning that it was violating a federal law forbidding the importation of creatures on the endangered species list. They singled out rattlesnakes from Pennsylvania.

I was sympathetic. Rattlesnakes weren't endangered in Idaho. I had spent much of my life trying to kill the damned things (unwisely, as it turns out), and it seemed to me like a classic case of bureaucratic intimidation and enforcement of meaningless regulations. I steamed into the Interior Department the next morning, made a few phone calls, and ordered the Fish and Wildlife Service guy who threatened Dominique to hold his fire. He didn't have the authority to write or issue threats. The rattlesnake wasn't yet officially listed as endangered.

It turned out, however, that the Fish and Wildlife Service knew how to send out a warning buzz in its own defense. An item soon appeared on the federal page of the *Washington Post* stating that I was trying to fire a lowly federal worker who was just doing his job. The cause was taken up by columnist Jack Anderson.

Cool it, advised my staff. I responded by getting stubborn. This guy had harassed my good friend Dominique. I was the interior secretary and I wanted him out.

All sorts of bad things began to happen. The press dug up the fact that we had listed for endangered species study a rattlesnake in New Mexico. Articles appeared on the shrinking habitat of the Eastern timber rattler. The Fish and Wildlife Service found that another possibly threatened creature, the dove, was being served to patrons at Dominique's. The agency began leaking information to a powerful congressman, Representative John Dingell, who chaired an investigations subcommittee and did not like me.

I flew off to California to dedicate the Santa Monica Mountains National Recreation Area. Microphones appeared, and a single subject dominated the questioning—rattlesnakes. My dinner at Dominique's had made it onto the network news. The next step would be that somebody would dub the controversy "Rattlegate" or "Vipergate."

I would have preferred dove at Dominique's, but it was time to eat crow. I put in a phone call to my press secretary and told him, "All right, I screwed up. Now get me out of it." The staff found a way. We referred the rattlesnake brouhaha to Bob Herbst, the assistant secretary who was overseer of the Fish and Wildlife Service. After a decent interval, he released a finding that the rattlesnake guy did not deserve to be fired. The press, which kind of liked me, did not strike further.

Whenever something like this comes up, I remember the example of a fellow Democratic governor also first elected in 1970, John Gilligan of Ohio, who got a little high-handed. During a visit to a farm or woolmaking operation, I forget which, Gilligan made a flip remark about how his job involved fleecing the taxpayers. He managed to get defeated in 1974, one of the best Democratic years of the century.

THE EXTRAVAGANCE FACTOR WAS PART OF THE REASON that, eighteen years later, another pair of Democratic governors went their separate ways. Bill Clinton was bound for New York to accept the Democratic presidential nomination. I saddled up a horse that week and went off into the Bitterroot Mountains on a pack trip with Idaho's national forest supervisors.

My disappearance was deliberate. I couldn't shake off my doubts about Clinton and didn't want to spend my breath denying them. He still reminded me of a high school student-body leader who desperately needed to be liked by everyone. I had premonitions that Clinton's character would rub Idaho voters the wrong way, with disastrous consequences for a Democratic Party striving to grow in harsh habitat. I kept quiet, but had my doubts borne out by the '92 election returns in my state and in the missteps of Clinton's first few months in the presidency.

The governor with the retinue named a White House staff bereft of people with gray hair and almost entirely lacking members from west of the Mississippi River and north of Los Angeles. Their first big issue was homosexuals in the military! They stumbled on Western issues like mining and grazing reform, listening to beltway environmentalists who wanted to punish states like mine for long-ago sins.

Clinton also began his term with wide eyes for the high perks of high office. He hung out with Barbra Streisand, enjoyed the famous two-hundred-dollar haircut at Los Angeles International Airport, and jetted off to high-gloss policy conferences called Renaissance Weekends at Hilton Head in South Carolina. Coupled with the Martha's Vineyard vacations and sailing trips with the Kennedys, it seemed to some like a presidential extension of the Xanadu effect.

The rough start might have been prevented had Clinton as governor not led such a protected life. He talked about Americans who work hard and play by the rules, but he never lived like one. The mansion, the troopers, the lure of being a celebrity clearly turned the head of the boy from Hope.

Clinton has, in part, grown out of his romance with perks, though. In 1995 and 1996, the sailing trips at Martha's Vineyard were replaced by vacations in the Tetons with river rafting and hikes on Mount Washburn in Yellowstone National Park. Still, the Clinton administration sometimes shows all the organization of a kindergarten class whose teacher has temporarily left the room. The high-handedness factor reemerged in the closing days of the '96 campaign, when high-roller fund-raising techniques caught up with Clinton's campaign and held the president's total to under 50 percent of the vote. In the summer of 1997, too, the Clintons went back to Martha's Vineyard.

If I had to offer Bill Clinton any advice for his remaining days in the White House, it would be what my dad told me when he first took me hunting: "You've got to keep your eye on the rabbit." It was a lesson for life. Don't get distracted with unimportant stuff. Keep your eyes on what you've set out to do. Never let your head get turned by your position. Power is temporary, and often illusory.

Chapter 3

TRIALS AND ERRORS

I MOVED TO WASHINGTON, D.C., IN 1977 knowing that I had won the trust of a fellow governor with whom I had served—Jimmy Carter. He had appointed me to his cabinet with the title of U.S. Secretary of the Interior. It remained for me to find the block-long Interior Department building at Eighteenth and C, win over the trust of those working there, and master public lands disputes that spanned a continent.

On the front burner were already-furious battles over whether to build more dams in the West and how much of Alaska to set aside as national parks and wildlife refuges. I did not have a precise agenda of where the administration was going, only a sense of what it needed to do. Jimmy Carter had won the presidency in 1976 with the electoral votes of only one state in the West—Hawaii. The Democratic president had to perform some bonding with a region that was trending Republican.

An administration can define or damage itself by actions taken in its earliest days. We were to define ourselves in the Alaska lands fight. But a damaging episode over dams and water came first. The same sort of self-inflicted wound would be repeated sixteen years later, the next time a Democrat won the presidency.

Carter had staffed the White House Council on Environmental Quality with a cadre of Washington, D.C.–based lobbyists from environmental groups. They were ready with an agenda, whether or not Carter and I were ready for them. They were bent on quickly achieving a longtime dream of the green lobby, shutting down U.S. Bureau of Reclamation water projects.

The administration's environmentalists did have sound economic arguments to make; they were challenging some very uneconomic projects. The Bureau of Reclamation was notorious for building dams that defied even the agency's own expansive definition of what was cost effective. BuRec's environmental destructiveness had inspired author Edward Abbey's nickname for the agency, the "U.S. Bureau of Wrecklamation."

Politically, however, the picture was different. The agency also had its accomplishments, its defenders, and a legacy of idealism. The Bureau of Reclamation had been launched with a mission to make deserts bloom. Several of its projects—Hoover Dam, Grand Coulee Dam, and Fort Peck Dam—were vital in shaping twentieth-century development of the American West. BuRec was a friend and benefactor to irrigators, an influential constituency in an arid region of the country.

Should axing reclamation projects be the early, defining agenda for an administration elected without support from the West? The question was already being answered before I had settled in at Eighteenth and C. White House environmentalists, led by Kathy Fletcher in the office of domestic policy adviser Stu Eizenstat, drew up a briefing book that contained a hit list of water projects marked for elimination. It included every project with a negative cost-benefit ratio.

A meeting was held in the cabinet room of the White House, Jimmy Carter presiding. I argued that we should use a scalpel instead of a meat-ax. Pick one or two really bad irrigation proposals—projects in which taxpayers would shell out millions to benefit a few dozen already-wealthy farmers—and use them to bring new accountability to the Bureau of Reclamation. This way, nobody could accuse us of waging a "war on the West." If we ganged up on every project, opponents would put together a coalition that would kick our butts.

The meeting ended without resolving the issue. I assumed that everyone would then make a case in writing to the president. Carter would go off alone, as was his wont, and make up his own mind. My assumptions were those of a novice in the wars of Washington, D.C. What the meeting did was set off alarms among hit-list proponents. They decided to force the issue.

Worried that the sweeping proposal would be watered down, they leaked their briefing book with the list of targeted projects to the press. As the Carter administration's chief public lands manager, I stepped off a plane in Denver to be met by a reporter holding the wire copy in his hand and asking for my comment.

The consequences were sad but predictable. Architects of the hit list had their story in the papers. In Congress, however, the Bureau of Reclamation had plenty of defenders with the power to block any elimination of water projects. The Carter administration was left looking weak, disorganized, and tone deaf toward a region of the country where it was already lacking support.

In another system of government, the situation would have played out differently, say if I had moved into No. 10 Downing Street in London or taken over a cabinet ministry in Ottawa. A permanent network of senior British or Canadian civil service mandarins would have been on hand to help shape my agenda—not bring in their own.

A new Canadian environment minister gave me cause for envy after his country changed governments in 1979. John Fraser and I had the foundations of affinity. He was a Westerner from British Columbia, a fanatical fly fisherman who had earned a nickname—"the Green Tory"—for his dedication to conservation. We were, however, also at odds. The Interior Department backed use of Port Angeles, Washington, as a receiving port for Alaska oil, which would then be shipped by pipeline across the continent. Canada wanted an all-land route that passed over Canadian soil and minimized tanker traffic off its west coast.

What amazed me, however, was that Fraser stood ready to deal and do battle from the moment of our first contact. He had gained familiarity with key issues while serving as his party's environment critic in the House of Commons. He took over a fully staffed government department that stood ready to receive directions. Frankly, I envied him.

WE IDAHOANS ALWAYS FELT A LITTLE BIT OUT OF PLACE in Washington, D.C. The town had its own kind of informal permanent government. Some of my administration colleagues, and many of their senior aides, had come to the city years earlier. They had risen along with each other. They had shuttled between private- and public-sector jobs. They were friends, lovers, colleagues, tennis partners—and, above all, networkers.

At a capital dinner party, the New Deal–vintage superlobbyist Tommy "the Cork" Corcoran asked Carol, "How do you like Washington, D.C.?"

"There are too many people, too many cars, and too much humidity in the summer," she replied.

Puzzled, Corcoran asked: "You do have air-conditioning, don't you?"

"We like to be outside in the summer," Carol responded.

Being bested by administration environmentalists in the early days of the Carter administration was a wake-up call. It was a seat-of-the-pants learning experience. I had to find out how to grasp the levers of power. In Washington, D.C., that often means getting the president's ear. Jimmy Carter, it turned out, loved blunt, concise decision memos, listing options along with advantages and disadvantages. The president took such materials along when he had to decide an issue. I made sure any piece of paper sent from the Interior Department to the White House quickly got to the point.

When I complained about interference with my department by White House aides who had never run for any kind of office, Carter sympathized. He gave me a personal phone number where I could reliably reach him at exactly 6:50 each evening. The number was stored away and used sparingly on occasions when I absolutely needed the all-powerful ear.

Such are the tactics of skirmishing in our democracy's capital. If you want to get anything done, you must go out and find like-minded, competent people who will share your trials and tribulations, and give direction to a permanent, bulky, and always-wary bureaucracy.

One of the better presidents that America never had, Adlai Stevenson, once observed that there are three principles of good management in government: Hire quality people. Tell them not to cut corners. And, when controversy arises, back them to the limit.

Stevenson was an idealist but managed to be both high-minded and a pretty effective governor of Illinois forty years ago. An opposite model in governing, perhaps, is provided by a deposed and deceased president, Richard Nixon, who continues to fascinate the country.

"You know, any effective leader has got to be a son of a bitch. . . . You have to instill the fear of God in your people to get results," Nixon growled to aide Monica Crowley, long after leaving office. Crowley tells this story in her book *Nixon off the Record*.

Curiously, Nixon in power was characterized by lack of interaction. He did not back anyone to the limit, nor did he face down or fire anybody. A palace guard kept away the cabinet officers and policy aides on which his success depended. The president would see the veterinarian treating his Irish setter, King Timahoe, but not his own secretary of defense.

I LEARNED BY TRIAL AND ERROR, NONE ANYWHERE near as grievous as Nixon's. Looking back on my days as a green-horn governor and unpolished cabinet secretary, I can now embrace Adlai Stevenson's principles and expand on them with some maxims of my own.

As governor, I prepared a standard admonition for those who came to work for me: Your name may be on the office door; my name goes on the ballot. I must ultimately answer for what you are doing. Ignorance does not excuse. I need to know what you are up to. Hand me a nasty surprise and I will hand you your head.

While laying down the law on that point, I tried never to put on airs. A political leader must give out loyalty and respect if he or she expects, in return, to receive it. Public service makes enormous demands on time, puts pressure on families, and is—with rare exceptions—no way to get rich. Decent human relationships, up and down the chain of command, become essential.

I made a point never to ask that an aide or department head do something that I would not do myself. There was to be no dishing out of the dirty work. Nor did public servants deserve to be treated as personal servants. I remember reading of one Minnesota congressman whose wife, a dog breeder, had aides take poodle pups to get their tails bobbed. He lost the respect of his staff, whose revelations to the *Washington Post* ultimately led to loss of his seat in Congress. Never would that type of stuff be allowed to happen in my shop.

In politics as in baseball, you have to tolerate a certain number of rookie errors. My first press secretary in the 1970s, John Hough, was a greenhorn television reporter. He was unprepared for the caution required on the other side of the microphone. On a fall hunting trip, I shot a three-point buck in Owyhee County. The deer had taken four bullets, but I had to cut the animal's throat to stop its thrashing. Hough thought the episode amusing and told a reporter. The headline was predictable: "Andrus Slays Bambi—Four Times!" On another occasion, my press secretary cited an ancient provision in Idaho's constitution under which Mormons could not vote. He used it as an example of an outmoded law that, while never repealed, simply was ignored. Again a sensational headline: "Andrus Says Mormons Unable to Vote by Idaho Constitution."

Urged to fire my press secretary, I declined. What purpose would it have served? Instead I moved him over to the management side of the office. He earned his stripes and later became my chief of staff. He went on to serve superbly in the Interior Department as my Western field director.

Given that my own tongue was getting me into plenty of trouble, punishing Hough also would have been an act of hypocrisy. I made an unfortunate reference to "the gun nuts of the world"—of which there are a goodly number in Idaho—and greeted the legislature's adjournment by saying how glad I was to see the fatheads leave town. Occasional bursts of irreverence have been part of my way of doing business. Speaking one's mind stirs controversy but is a way of staying sane.

I did my own hiring and firing in key positions. Good sense demands that you size up people on whom your success in office depends. I find it amazing to this day that Ronald Reagan met for only about fifteen minutes with the man who would be my successor as interior secretary, James Watt, before handing him a sensitive cabinet portfolio. Jimmy Carter knew me well and we had talked about the Interior Department and public lands policy at length. Still, he took three hours to go over the job.

When it comes time to sever a relationship, cut and cut quickly—and do the cutting yourself. A clean wound heals quickest. The ousted aide or department head will not feel abused.

Remember the lesson of Donald Regan. One afternoon in 1987, the embattled White House chief of staff tuned in his office TV set to learn that Howard Baker had just been hired to take his place. No resignation letter had been requested. President Reagan had delivered no hints, although first lady Nancy Reagan was waging war on Regan using the weapon of news leaks. Less than a year later, with the Gipper still in office, Don Regan would wield a slashing sword of retribution. He published memoirs revealing, among other things, that Nancy Reagan encouraged an astrologer to exercise control over her husband's schedule.

As governor and interior secretary, I tried always to "hire up," enduring the risk of potential rejection to find and lure the people I wanted. Often it took a lot of persuasion. When I began my second tenure as governor in 1987, our state's economy had tanked out in the recession that hit mining and timber in the early 1980s.

The state Department of Commerce was key. I went to work on a successful Republican businessman named Jim Hawkins to become its director. Luckily, for me as persuader, the man loved Idaho and had a conscience. He was one of those people who had made a bundle and felt obligated to give something back. He was just the right person to have as a recruiter at a time when the West was beginning to be recognized as the gateway to the most dynamic, fastest-growing trade region of the world—Asia.

I had to demonstrate, as well, the governor's firing power. In politics, a problem that is allowed to fester begins quickly to stink. Worst of all, it can make you look like a public hypocrite.

As governor, I had made a big deal out of refusing police protection and sending state troopers back out on the road to arrest speeders. The lack of protection, the absence of special treatment for the governor, became a kind of hallmark of my second tenure in the statehouse. But just a week before the 1990 election, it was revealed that the state Department of Law Enforcement was practicing favoritism. The troopers were back on the road, but they were being told to refrain from ticketing legislators, state officials, and prominent citizens.

I cussed up a storm in private, and delivered the public promise, "I will personally look into this and deal with it myself." The promise was closely watched. I flew around Idaho, asking at each stop to speak with rank-and-file state police officers. They looked me in the eye and told me what I dreaded hearing. All had been given the same instruction: "There are certain people you've got to be lenient with—mayors, legislators, and brothers in law enforcement."

I flew back to Boise and confronted the state law enforcement director. He denied favoritism. I knew better. I fired him just two days after the election. What a helluva way to begin one's final term in office, but I laid out the reason: "I will not tolerate, nor will the people of Idaho tolerate, any policy of special treatment toward anyone."

YEARS BEFORE, IN THE EARLY 1970S, AT THE BEHEST OF a talented young aide, Larry Meierotto, I inaugurated a program called Capitol for a Day. During the year, I would hold public meetings and spend time in every county seat of Idaho's forty-four counties. I would walk the streets of a community, dropping in on small businesses. Into a drugstore I would go, asking the owner, "Are you getting decent treatment in your dealing with state government?"

This was an exercise in effective governing, but it was also effective politicking. I wanted to stay in office. To do so it was necessary to get unfiltered data on what the voters were thinking and their impressions of how state government was serving them. Polls and cross-tabulations were, thank goodness, still in the future. I did my own polling. I learned a heckuva lot more from folks who came to my meetings than they ever learned from me.

The people I met on these trips, main-streeting and talking at luncheons, could usually be divided into quartiles. About 25 percent of those who showed up were people who needed the services of psychiatric medicine. Another 25 percent were folks who could use a lawyer. The third quarter were those who would come to gripe. And the final quartile were people with legitimate complaints and concerns.

All required listening, even the eccentrics. Once, in Grangeville, I heard—loudly—from a fellow named Buckskin Billy, a Salmon River hermit. The U.S. Forest Service was about to evict him. Buckskin Billy would have none of it. He wanted me, on the spot, to write out a deed for the federal property on which he lived. When I wouldn't provide immediate relief, Billy got personal and insulting. It was one of the few times in my life that I almost threw a punch at a constituent. My press secretary, Chris Carlson, said later that he saw my face flush and thought, "Uh-oh. He's going to deck this guy, and the headline won't be pretty."

While I'm no paragon of restraint, I did repress my first impulse and allowed as how Billy ought to turn around and head back down the street. Such encounters were rare. The trick at luncheons or town meetings was not to let the Buckskin Billys dominate. I developed a talent for shutting up obnoxious people and, if necessary, showing them the door. The professional gripers I greeted with the question, "Are you registered to vote?" Often they were not active participants in the democratic process.

In particular, I trained myself to encourage and hear out those people with a valid beef. They usually had received a brushoff from some lower level of the bureaucracy. The right of appeal applies in government as well as the courts. A citizen should always have the opportunity to take his or her case to a higher level.

I would go through a Capitol-for-a-Day schedule and hand out cards like a Las Vegas blackjack dealer. Write down your problem, I would tell people. You will get a call. You will be taken seriously. And back in Boise, I made sure of it. The cards were passed out to staff and cabinet heads. The instruction was to get at least a preliminary answer to these questions, in language the citizen could understand, within two weeks.

Getting around and making that sort of contact is possible in a state with only 1.2 million people. I could hear feedback on how people's questions were handled just by going into small-town cafes, drinking industrial-strength coffee, and getting an earful. The best questions were what some in the media might describe as unimportant or "bite-size": The agricultural extension service wasn't helping farmers get barrier trees anymore; the rural bookmobile didn't stop on the road between St. Maries and Potlatch Junction.

Unimportant, hell! We get powerful winter winds in northern Idaho. Barrier trees for windbreaks are important in shielding farm buildings. We've seen small timber and mining towns lose population. Those hanging on, or moving in, tend to be senior citizens. Having access to a bookmobile is an important part of rural life.

Town meetings were a device for keeping state government accountable. State-of-the-state speeches proved a very different tool, a chance to give an accounting and set direction. Such speeches are events that cause even nonpolitical folks to tune into their government. I was acutely aware of people's short attention spans when it came to public policy. My constituency never consisted of Ph.D.'s. Instead, I won four statewide elections thanks to folks who carried lunch buckets and drove pickup trucks.

Perhaps the best advice I ever received on giving speeches came in a slow drawl from Texas Governor Ann Richards during a National Governors' Association meeting. A long-winded position paper was on the table. Gazing up from her bifocals, Richards said, "My momma won't understand this. And if my momma doesn't understand it, nobody will. Put this in language my momma will understand."

State-of-the-state speeches carried messages for opinion makers, but I wanted myself understood at roadside cafes. Certain messages, on subjects like nuclear waste, had to travel beyond state lines. But for the ordinary citizens, I had to answer two questions: Did I understand their problems? Would proposals in the speech make their lives a little bit easier or improve the education of their kids?

We're talking Politics 101, but you'd be surprised who flunks. George Bush had been a global leader in the Gulf War, and the nation waited to see what he would do on the domestic front. A visionless 1992 State of the Union speech may have doomed his presidency. Bill Clinton's lengthy 1995 and 1996 speeches were dismissed by scornful Washington, D.C., pundits. Later polls showed, however, that Clinton still managed to connect with ordinary voters through down-to-earth proposals like boosting the minimum wage and expanding family leave.

SOME OTHER GOOD ADVICE ON POLITICS CAME DURING my first race for governor when Boise banker Bob Montgomery looked me in the eye and told me, "Never make the same mistake twice." I should have introduced Bob to Bill Clinton. Heeding Montgomery's maxim might have prevented Clinton's new administration from making the same kind of mistake that plagued Carter. For Clinton, the difficult issues of the West were mining and grazing.

We had five Democratic governors in the Mountain West when Clinton took office. A group of us went to work on a deal to boost grazing fees charged on federal lands in the West and require more conservation-sensitive range management. Millions of acres, mostly handled by the Bureau of Land Management, are overgrazed and have suffered resulting erosion damage and loss of wildlife habitat. Wealthy corporations and individuals pay rock-bottom rates to run their sheep and cattle on public land.

I also worked with Wyoming Governor Mike Sullivan to get a compromise on a reform of the 1872 Mining Law, under which federal land worth billions of dollars has been turned over to mining companies for a pittance. We won informal agreement from mining folks that the archaic law needed reform and that the industry would have to make more concessions than required in the phony "reform" bills sponsored by its allies in Congress.

In both cases, we ran into Council on Environmental Quality boss Katie McGinty. She was a White House insider and former aide to Vice President Al Gore. She wanted more concessions and was loath to yield control of the issue to people in faraway state-houses. We were told by the White House there would be no deal. In turn, Congress blocked the administration's plans. Clinton was willing to abandon mining and grazing reform as a price for getting votes for his economic package.

The upshot? Interior Secretary Bruce Babbitt was derided by environmental activists for selling out, and made into a devil figure by conservative groups for advocating reform in the first place. The Mining Law of 1872 stayed on the books. I'm convinced that, with governors in the lead, we could have gotten 90 percent of the Clinton administration's proposed mining reforms enacted into law, and maybe 75 percent of what they wanted on rangeland management. An early victory would have signaled that this Democratic administration was sensitive to the West and able to wisely compromise.

With mines and grazing in 1993, as with water projects in 1977, absolutists in the environmental camp would not settle for three-quarters of the pie. So they ended up going hungry. They also lost political allies who would at least give them a place at the dinner table. Republicans captured the Idaho, Wyoming, and New Mexico statehouses in 1994. Mike Sullivan lost a Senate race in Wyoming.

A director of the Council on Environmental Quality, or a bureaucratic infighter at the Office of Management and Budget, can brilliantly manipulate a White House decision. Still, they aren't answerable out at the roadside restaurants, and they aren't the people who have to hear out the angry cattle ranchers.

I've found that being out there on the ballot teaches lessons that no mandarin in a capital office will ever learn: Always strive for a win-win situation. Work out a compromise in which credit is shared, even if one side is backing down. And recognize needs of the other party.

One episode demonstrates the art of the political deal. During my first term as governor, the Perrine Bridge over the Snake River near Twin Falls was in danger of falling down. The state had no money to replace it. I cast a covetous eye toward federal highway trust funds. The key to the vault lay in the possession of John Volpe, Nixon's transportation secretary and a former Massachusetts governor.

Volpe was a peppy, bombastic little guy forever on the outs with the dour Prussians who ran the White House. He was also, I recall, in hot water over one of those trivial controversies that people talk about at Washington, D.C., dinner parties and about which the rest of the country could give a damn.

On a trip to Washington, D.C., I literally lay in ambush for Volpe and Interior Secretary Rogers Morton. Morton knew me and gave a warm greeting, excuse enough for me to jump into Volpe's limousine. Volpe was uptight, but quickly caught on to what I was proposing. The deal was a bridge in exchange for a billboard. Highway beautification was a popular cause of the time. Volpe was under fire for not taking it seriously. Once he agreed to the new bridge, the transportation secretary was invited to transport himself out to Idaho. With TV cameras rolling, John Volpe was given the opportunity to chainsaw a big, eye-polluting billboard. Volpe beamed with pleasure. He made the national news, I had a friend in high places, and Twin Falls had a new bridge.

ECONOMIST-AMBASSADOR JOHN KENNETH GALBRAITH wrote a wonderful memoir called *A Life in Our Times*. A friend pointed out to me one of Galbraith's rules for getting things done in government: Cultivate a modest aspect of menace.

Menace often produces movement. A colleague, Governor Tom McCall of Oregon, once plunked down a helicopter on the Oregon coast, marched onto a stretch of sand claimed by a developer, glowered at a partially built fence, and vowed it would be torn down. The scene was a key move in McCall's successful crusade to thwart those who wanted to block access to Oregon's beaches. The public stand galvanized the state and pushed reluctant legislators to action.

In Olympia, oil industry lobbyists tied up Washington Governor Dan Evans's efforts to enact a clean air and clean water package and create a state agency charged with environmental protection. Evans resorted to a statewide television appeal for his environmental package. The legislation broke free on a wave of public support. The following November, voters ended the careers of several lawmakers who had blocked it.

My time to draw a line in the sand came on the issue of nuclear waste. I had resolved, and promised voters, that the U.S. Department of Energy would not continue to use Idaho as a dumping ground for radioactive material from its Rocky Flats, Colorado, nuclear weapons plant. The department, and its predecessor the Atomic Energy Commission, had made and broken promises to me about wastes already on the Idaho National Engineering and Environmental Laboratory reservation. The existing wastes had been mishandled.

In order to deliver on my no-dumping pledge, we needed to dislodge one of the most obstinate bureaucracies in Washington, D.C., the nuclear weapons overseers. We deployed a three-step strategy: Try reason first. Then send a lawyer to the federal courthouse. And, lastly, send an unmistakable message that would be seen far beyond the Forrestal Building, the Department of Energy headquarters in Washington, D.C.

The unmistakable message finally came in the form of an Idaho State Police officer standing on the railroad tracks in front of a nuclear waste shipment. His picture appeared on the front page of the *New York Times*. We were *not* going to take any more stuff from Rocky Flats. The governor of Colorado blinked and took back the waste shipment. The Department of Energy came to the bargaining table and signed a memorandum of understanding.

Environmental threats are a good place to draw lines and send messages. When I get impatient with preservationists, there are some battle ribbons I can show them. The Pioneer power plant battle gives me satisfaction more than two decades after it was fought.

The Idaho Power Company was so powerful a presence in the early 1970s that wags joked that they named a state after it. The company was wedded to bigness. Having erected three dams in Hells Canyon, and forecasting that power demand would continue to climb at a rate of about 7 percent a year, it planned to build a big coal-burning power plant called Pioneer at a site near Boise. The company lined up support from the usual suspects—agribusiness, unthinking chambers of commerce, job-hungry construction unions, and a bevy of Republican politicians. What it had not counted on was a governor who could ask tough questions.

Designed without scrubbers to remove impurities from plant emissions, and located only thirty miles away from the state capital, Pioneer would have made Boise a far less attractive place to live. Doctors told us it could cause respiratory problems downwind. By pushing up power costs, it would hold down the power use that justified its construction in the first place. The power plant was unhealthy for stockholders as well as ratepayers.

Pioneer would have been built had we not stopped it. Stopping it involved a curious and convoluted flow of information. Insiders at Idaho Power fed data on potential impacts and questionable economic assumptions to the governor's office. They feared that a hidebound senior management couldn't fathom the plant's costs or its impact on the company. The insider stuff, in turn, was used to educate the Idaho Public Utility Commission. The commission was not accustomed to dealing with people's breathing problems or standing in the way of either growth or the Idaho Power Company.

The education was accomplished with a little help from the governor's office. I decided to go before a commission hearing and testify. To two of the three commissioners, my presence was an in-the-flesh reminder of who had appointed them. In short order, they developed a whole new way of looking at things, becoming aware of impacts on the environment and potentially higher power rates. Pioneer was rejected.

If I were to look for a symbol of government's old way of doing business, I'd probably pick a big manmade pile of dirt that sat for seventeen years at the city limits of Wallace, Idaho. Interstate 90 was to be routed right through the heart of this colorful old mining town. The freeway project would have destroyed at least half of the historic hamlet in Idaho's northern panhandle. Of course, there was no need to blast right through the town, but that's how the state Highway Board and the Federal Highway Administration thought at the time. About three hundred miles away, at the western terminus of I-90, they were proposing to do exactly the same thing to a historic Seattle neighborhood.

Wallace became an opportunity to use the National Environmental Policy Act and other new laws passed in the early 1970s. The highwaymen never knew what hit them. They had never met a fellow like Harry Magnuson, the entrepreneur whose ideas for recreation and tourism saved Wallace when the mines shut down.

I sat down recently with Harry, who beams at memories of the good fight. "We stopped the goddamned highway, and it took seventeen years to get it going again," he said. During that time, highway traffic had to slow down: Wallace had the only traffic light on the interstate between Seattle and Boston. Eventually, the highwaymen were forced to move their project back to the slopes of a hill just north of town. Having circled the wagons, the bureaucracy eventually had to move—literally—in a different direction.

I take great pride in the learning I did by the seat of my pants. Of course, there were trials and errors, like failing to rein in the Council on Environmental Quality's desire to go ahead with its hit list of water projects. Still, I can dine at Harry Magnuson's hotel in Wallace, with the freeway safely out of town. I can walk my dog on a hillside park above Boise without inhaling a coal plant's sulfur dioxide. I can look at former aides who started out in my shop. Now prosperous in business, they still—as citizens—are giving of their skills to preserve the wild Hanford Reach of the Columbia River and to get salmon-destroying dams removed from the Elwha River on Washington's Olympic Peninsula. They work as watchdogs for places like Hells Canyon, where exploiters still lurk.

The satisfactions must largely be personal. While finding new mistakes to make, I did adhere to Montgomery's maxim about not making the same error twice. The continued friendship of most former aides indicates that I followed Adlai Stevenson's advice about backing them up. I can still walk into roadside diners and run into people who used Capitol for a Day to settle a beef with government. And while we never did get used to the summers, I learned how to get things done at that big building at Eighteenth and C in Washington, D.C.

Chapter 4

LESSONS FROM A SELF-TAUGHT CONSERVATIONIST

W HEN CONGRESS APPROVED THE 103-million-acre Alaska Lands Act in President Carter's waning days in office in 1980, a lame-duck administration was briefly able to look like a swan. However tarnished his record may have appeared, Carter managed to leave behind a legacy of volcanic craters, alpine lakes, ancient forests, tundras needed by grizzly bears, and federal land managers who weren't devoted only to drilling, digging up, and cutting down the great resources of America's forty-ninth state.

At the time, nobody gave Jimmy Carter credit, or seemed to notice. Alas, the legacy was located just about as far from Washington, D.C., as you can go in America, and worlds away from the movers and shakers of our capital. Only one capital pundit, political cartoonist Pat Oliphant, consistently drew on the issue. Alaska and the West had yet to become one of America's "hot" places to live or visit.

Those days crystallized my impatience toward the town in which I had labored as secretary of the interior for four years. The media was filled with reports of Ronald and Nancy Reagan's arrival and their observance of the rituals of social courtship that the Carters had shunned. A dinner party for the Gipper at Katharine Graham's mansion merited exhaustive coverage. Who cared if down at Carter's White House, the size of the national park system was being doubled?

The Alaska Lands Act was signed in the East Room of the White House in December 1980. I watched a tired and drawn Carter arrive for the signing ceremony. Then, for a moment as he acknowledged the applause—perhaps the last such moment of his presidency—Carter became relaxed and expansive. The color came back to his face.

The rap on Carter, endlessly circulated in press reports and capital chatter, was that he was mean without being tough. The assessment was wrong on both counts: Trust the testimony of somebody who, as a cabinet member, watched him for four years. Carter was never a glad-hander. He guarded his privacy. The president's pale blue eyes occasionally would fix on someone and register dissatisfaction without a word being spoken. As a friend he was considerate, however, and as a boss he was somebody who shared in the heavy lifting. I needed his help, big time, in pushing the largest land conservation initiative in American history.

The key action that produced the White House signing ceremony had come two years earlier. Negotiations in Congress for a bill creating parks and wildlife refuges in Alaska had broken down. A moratorium on development was about to expire, opening vast areas of proposed parkland to activities that might preclude preservation. The administration, as the key player in the conservation battle, had to show that it meant business.

I approached Carter with the then-seventy-year-old Antiquities Act, a law that gave the president authority to proclaim national monuments on federal land. Theodore Roosevelt had used it to protect the Grand Canyon and Death Valley. Laying out a map of Alaska, I recommended to the president that he proclaim as national monuments the parks we had proposed. In this way, he would at least set aside fifty-six million acres and protect places from the Gates of the Arctic portion of the Brooks Range in the far north to the Misty Fjords area at the south end of the Alaska Panhandle.

"Can I do that?" Carter asked, incredulous that here was a domestic issue on which the president could decisively act.

"You have the authority, sir," I responded.

"Let's do it," he said.

Proclamation of the monuments caused enormous yelping, as would President Clinton's designation of the Escalante–Grand

Staircase National Monument in Utah eighteen years later. Developers were precluded from the familiar tactic of nibbling away at proposed parklands. A court action against Carter's proclamation was filed. At the Alaska State Fair, some folks lined up and paid to throw bottles at a likeness of me.

The proclamation worked as a political tactic. A decision on whether to set aside a portion of America's last frontier, in its natural state, could not be delayed to death. The opponents of large-scale land preservation were brought back to the bargaining table, the hostile presidential action driving them to strike a deal. They would eventually have to agree to a sweeping settlement that turned Carter's national monuments into national parks and protected millions more acres as wildlife refuges, wild and scenic rivers, and wilderness areas.

A KEY SKIRMISH IN THE BATTLE OVER ALASKA HAD also taken place in the Carter cabinet. In northern Alaska, I championed creation of an Arctic National Wildlife Refuge that would protect the full migrating range of the Porcupine Caribou Herd, perhaps the greatest concentration of hooved mammals in North America. Absolutely essential to this goal was preserving calving grounds along the Beaufort Sea. Here was where caribou had their calves, and where they escaped one of the world's fiercest concentrations of mosquitoes. Wolves and grizzlies, in turn, depended on the calving for a supply of meat. The natural food chain was undisturbed.

The coastal plain near the Beaufort Sea was, however, a place where oil and gas producers wanted to drill. They talked of discovering oil reserves that would equal or surpass those of Prudhoe Bay to the west, which had caused the Alaska pipeline to be built and were the foundation of the state's wealth. It was, and is, a question of values. I was aware that the industry's own calculation of the odds against discovering oil in quantities that were economically recoverable stood at four to one. Whatever oil we found would satisfy a few months' or at most a year's worth of the nation's insatiable demand for petroleum, at an environmental cost that was potentially enormous.

Secretary of Energy James Schlesinger took a different view. This was the eve of the world's second great oil crunch. The shah was being toppled in Iran. Schlesinger talked incessantly of an impending crisis and argued with conviction for the goal of energy independence. The Alaska debate would flare up in cabinet sessions. I would make a pitch for the refuge. "Yes, but we have a great wealth of oil that we will be unable to get to," Schlesinger would reply. "There is a storehouse of BTUs [British thermal units] beneath the tundra."

Carter would appear to have resolved the matter by saying, "I'm going with Cece on this one."

Of course, nothing was resolved, in the cabinet or later in Congress. The Alaska Lands Act contained a Solomonic compromise. A nineteen-million-acre Arctic National Wildlife Refuge came into being. But only eight million acres were classified as wilderness, permanently precluding oil and gas exploration. The coastal plain was left out of the wilderness designation. Assessments of its oil potential were authorized. Congress was given the final decision on whether to allow drilling. It was a formula for never-ending conflict. Nearly two decades later, the oil industry and environmentalists are still locked in combat over the caribou calving grounds.

LOOKING BACK, I'M AMAZED AT HOW MUCH WE WERE
able to do. I called on Carter consistently; whatever the world's
crises at the moment, he put out the requested effort. He backed
me in the cabinet. He proclaimed the national monuments. He
made calls to Congress. He listened politely to an emotional
appeal from Alaska Senator Ted Stevens, who argued that his
state's economic development would be hamstrung by a big parks
bill. As a power on the Senate Appropriations Committee,
Stevens could offer any number of deals to the president.

The Georgian had a genuine feel for preservation on a big
scale, however, and of what is meant by long-term legacy. Carter
was also willing to challenge the Western notion of "frontier" as
synonymous with exploitation and to set parameters of preservation before public lands were committed to development.

Long-term legacy is tough to think of in the pressure cooker
of Washington, D.C. The capital's culture so often reminds me of
a major league baseball team that is pressured to win this year's
pennant by trading away its future talent. Always there are
budget bills to be passed. Carter had energy proposals, from oil
shale development to filling the nation's petroleum reserve, that
were stalled in a Congress run by his own party. Yet he would not
deal away the long-term future of wild, faraway lands in order to
realize immediate gain.

The forty-ninth state was, and is, our country's last frontier.
So much of the American West was settled in a head-over-heels
fashion during the late nineteenth century. Immense land grants
were given to railroads, leading to the huge timber clear-cuts of
the late twentieth century. By the end of the nineteenth century,
however, buffalo had been exterminated. Millions of acres were
overgrazed, so badly that Theodore Roosevelt was writing angry
letters from the Dakotas as early as the 1880s.

Alaska was our one last chance to do things right, to recognize for once that the highest and best use for a big chunk of America's frontier was not "taming" but protection. Alaska had not fared all that well in the first century after its purchase from Russia in 1867. It was seen only as a place to be exploited. Boom and bust was the rule. Resources were seized upon and decimated. Fur seals were hunted to the brink of extinction, salmon runs were overfished, and minerals were gouged from the earth with abandon.

In the curious way that epic decisions get made, the impetus to preserve nearly a third of Alaska was provided by discovery of oil at Prudhoe Bay and the challenge of moving it to market. After much debate, a so-called all-American pipeline became the chosen transport route. It would carry crude oil from Prudhoe Bay to Valdez in southern Alaska, whereupon it would be shipped by tanker—without risk, the oil companies assured everyone—to the "Lower 48." But environmental disputes pressed on the pipeline, along with the genuine moral concern that Americans not replicate another wrong of the nineteenth century—the brutal displacement of aboriginal peoples.

A wise predecessor of mine, Interior Secretary Stewart Udall, had moved in 1966 to freeze all disposition of land claims in Alaska pending settlement of claims by the state's native peoples. The action stopped homesteading and kept the state of Alaska from completing the acquisition of 104 million federal acres that it was guaranteed upon statehood in 1959.

The resolution of native land issues became a necessary prelude to building the pipeline, or getting anything else done in Alaska. Udall's action prompted Congress to pass a landmark law for Native Americans, the Alaska Native Claims Settlement Act, which in turn led to the great conservation act that President Carter signed in the East Room. The claims settlement act, passed in 1971, gave legal rights to Alaska's native peoples and divided the state into twelve native regional corporations, which received land according to historic patterns of use. A thirteenth corporation represented natives in urban areas. In this way, natives were apportioned forty-four million acres of "the Great Land," in addition to receiving almost $1 billion.

The claims legislation included, deep in its legal language, section 17:d(2), which decreed that at least eighty million acres of "national interest" lands be set aside for protection based on their natural features. These were the lands I would refer to (endlessly, according to my staff) as "the crown jewels of Alaska." The Nixon and Ford administrations did not give great priority to working out what lands would be preserved. The task would eventually fall to Jimmy Carter, and to the onetime gyppo logger he appointed to be interior secretary.

The state and natives had made their land claims to Alaska. But development interests and their allies seemed to want open season on all federal, state, and tribal lands. The Great Land's politicians dreamed of the same rush to mine and log and drill that had swept across the rest of the West. Asked what places deserved protection, one developer would tell the *Seattle Post-Intelligencer* that national parks were fine as long as they were located "above 12,000 feet."

A canny and moderate Alaska politician of the era, two-term GOP Governor Jay Hammond, would later characterize his state's gung-ho developers as "propeller-heads." Hammond explained in his memoirs that one major challenge in seeking a reasonable solution to Alaska's land controversies was reining in unreasonable people.

SOME FOLKS WOULD LIVE UP TO HAMMOND'S NICKNAME. We heard arguments that moose love mines. Clear-cuts would improve the view so bald eagles could better spot their prey. Pulp mill effluent provided a warm habitat for salmon. The mind-set is symbolized in an immortal remark by another governor who became interior secretary, Alaskan Walter J. Hickel, who declared: "We can't just let nature run wild."

Behind the rhetoric flowed a gusher of dollars. Oil companies and miners poured resources into a classic industry lobbying campaign. Some of it was candid: U.S. Borax made clear its desire to build a big mine in the heart of Misty Fjords. But there was also a phony citizens movement that made way-out claims of potential economic damage to Alaska. The goal was to reduce the size and undermine the purposes of proposed national parks. One mining company wanted to build a road across major wildlife migration routes in the planned Gates of the Arctic National Park. Wildlife would adapt, we were told. They would have to adapt.

In some places, however, nature should still run wild. Some creatures—grizzlies come to mind—do not easily share space with two-legged intruders. In the Brooks Range, a barren-ground grizzly bear needs to range over as much as one hundred thousand acres of land.

We also heard a lot of phony characterizations of those who would enjoy these protected public lands. Parks would be the domain of the "effete rich," declared Senator Stevens. "Jet-setting hippie backpackers" were the only group that could afford to see his state's wonderlands, argued Alaska Representative Don Young.

From generation to generation, and from place to place, America's preservation battles have featured similar false claims.

In the early 1940s, opponents argued that creation of a national park in the Teton Range of Wyoming would devastate the local economy, then based on ranching. Critics held that Franklin D. Roosevelt was committing a giant waste of timber when he put nine hundred thousand acres of Washington's Olympic Mountains, including rain-forest valleys, into a national park. Today, of course, Grand Teton and Olympic National Parks are among the nation's premier travel destinations. President Clinton has twice vacationed at Grand Teton National Park.

Similarly, in Alaska, dire predictions accompanied the creation or expansion of ten national parks. But the great green splotches of parks on tourist maps intrigued would-be visitors and have attracted thousands of people to the Great Land. In the late 1970s, nobody could foresee that within twenty years the state capital of Juneau would play host to five hundred thousand cruise ship passengers a year. Or that many would peel off the regular tourist path to watch bears in Admiralty Island National Monument, or take boats up Tracy Arm in a nearby wilderness area. The town of Seward has prospered as a gateway to the seal and bird rookeries of Kenai Fjords National Park.

Even back in 1980, however, people seemed to sense the value of what we were doing, although it would be years—if ever—before they would ever see such wild places. Americans had made a headlong rush in the nineteenth century to exploit their land. They were, by the late twentieth century, of a mood not to repeat the excesses of yesterday. We may have been fighting powerful lobbies, but public opinion stood with us. I received countless letters, from schoolkids as well as seniors, arguing that caribou herds and wolves in Alaska should not be allowed to go the way of the passenger pigeon or Plains buffalo.

I grew attached to places we were fighting to preserve.

Admiralty Island, west of Juneau, is home to the nation's densest concentrations of brown bears and nesting bald eagles. In the 1950s, however, its forests were viewed by the U.S. Forest Service only as a source of wood chips. A big pulp mill was planned near Juneau, with its lucky owner to get a fifty-year timber supply contract. Uncle Sam would have subsidized the logging roads. A lawsuit stopped the contract and set the stage for our fight to preserve the million-acre island.

The Brooks Range in northern Alaska is a wildland with vertical granite walls to rival Yosemite, lakes with the world's finest fly-fishing, and concentrations of wildlife reminiscent of what Lewis and Clark saw as they crossed the Great Plains. Big-scale country, even compared with Idaho, the Gates of the Arctic took my breath away when I saw it in 1978.

Stewart Udall had primed Lyndon Johnson to proclaim a national monument in the heart of the Brooks Range just before Johnson left the White House in 1969. The papers were on the president's desk. Udall, however, committed an unpardonable sin against Johnson's psyche. He renamed the Washington, D.C., football stadium after Robert F. Kennedy. Johnson refused to sign off on the monument. The Brooks Range became a football in the epic American feud between LBJ and the Kennedys. Once again, action had to await the Alaska Lands Act.

Don Young would become chairman of the House Resources Committee when Republicans took control of Congress in 1995. He acted like an unrepentant propeller-head, having the committee take up legislative proposals to expand hunting in Alaska national parks and to cut more trees around those places in southeast Alaska that we managed to preserve. He succeeded only in bringing down an avalanche of negative publicity on the Alaska congressional delegation. The forty-ninth state had, at last, been discovered.

The Interior Department and its secretary get only periodic attention. Albert Fall went to jail in the 1920s. Harold Ickes was a strong man in Roosevelt's cabinet. James Watt was a public relations disaster under Reagan, and a boon to the membership-hungry environmental groups that fought his policies. The Sierra Club had 179,000 members when I handed control of the Interior Department to Watt. By the time Nancy Reagan had engineered his removal in 1983, the club's membership topped 350,000.

Unlike the secretary of state or attorney general, I was not immediately confronted with a list of the world's hot spots or faced with a decision on what to do about the ethical lapses of one of the president's closest friends. The Interior Department was overseer of a vast domain, but was rarely seen in Washington, D.C.'s media frenzy.

The department had been pretty well neutered over the previous ten years. Walter Hickel was outspoken on many fronts after President Nixon gave him the Interior Department job in 1969. He was unceremoniously fired in 1970. The lesson was not lost on his successors, who did not stick their necks out or do anything to attract much notice.

JIMMY CARTER WAS, WITH THEODORE ROOSEVELT, ONE of the two most committed conservationists ever to occupy the Oval Office. He did not treat nature as a photo opportunity. After the administration's initial stumble over its hit list of water projects, he actively backed me up. As preludes to the Alaska battle, we were able to get Congress to pass a Surface Mining Act, requiring that mined-over land be replanted and reclaimed. The Interior Department was charged with enforcing the law. We created a bidding mechanism for coal mining leases on federal land and put environmental provisions into offshore leasing.

The Interior Department was a player, which in the last days of Carter's presidency was a crucial factor in getting an Alaska Lands Act signed into law. We needed to get the issue resolved while Carter was still in office. Ronald Reagan was certainly not going to "lock up"—to use a favorite term of his supporters—a quarter of the nation's largest state.

In 1978 and again in 1980, the two houses of Congress had passed two very different Alaska lands bills, under auspices of two very different architects. The House of Representatives, over shouted opposition from Don Young, passed sweeping legislation containing every acre we wanted and then some. Overseeing the bill was Representative Morris Udall, chairman of the House Interior Committee and one of the remarkable conservationists of our time.

Mo Udall saw the opportunity for preservation in Alaska and nurtured it. He appointed a soft-spoken but fearless congressman, John Seiberling, to chair hearings on what and how much to preserve. Udall and Seiberling made sure everybody was heard, not just the drums that were banging loudest. In the case of southeast Alaska, the subcommittee heard not only the Louisiana-Pacific Corporation, which wanted to log everywhere within economical reach of its Ketchikan, Alaska, mill, but also operators of small fishing lodges on Prince of Wales Island whose livelihood was threatened by rapid clear-cutting of their island home. With such groundwork laid, a conservationist Alaska lands package rolled over a rival proposal by a one-hundred-vote margin on the House floor.

The Senate, by contrast, preserved almost as much land, but also kept open a variety of development opportunities. It excised the coastal plain of the Arctic National Wildlife Refuge from wilderness designation. A hole was left in the wilderness portion of Misty Fjords National Monument to make room for U.S. Borax and its planned molybdenum mine.

The Senate bill was crafted by two shrewd legislative barons, Democratic Senator Henry Jackson of Washington and Alaska's Ted Stevens. "Scoop" Jackson was a friend of mine. He had helped get me elected governor of Idaho in 1970. He was a visionary, author of the National Environmental Policy Act, and liked to rumble at young environmentalists, "I was a conservationist before you were born."

Scoop was, however, shaped by the World War II experience. He never forgot the lessons of Munich, seeing an America forever in danger from Soviet military might. Nor did he forget that Japan had cut off America's rubber supply when it captured the Dutch East Indies in 1942. Jackson spent much of the 1970s giving long, boring speeches about America's growing dependence on foreign oil. We should have listened to him, but didn't.

In Alaska, Jackson saw the need for conservation—but also oil reserves and minerals that the country might need in an emergency. He was also a buddy of the first secretary of energy, James Schlesinger. As a result, Jackson crafted a bulky beast of a bill. The legislation didn't throw open the doors to development, but left open the future possibility. Its provisions created years of employment opportunities for Washington, D.C., lobbyists.

Stevens saw Jackson's bill as the best he could get. The Indianapolis-born, Harvard-trained lawyer was one of the orneriest adversaries I was ever to face across the bargaining table. He had gone to Alaska as an Interior Department lawyer in the 1950s, and came back to Washington, D.C., as a U.S. senator in 1968. He has since considered himself Alaska's ambassador to an uncomprehending America. Ted championed military bases, public works projects, and oil companies.

In 1978, just before Carter proclaimed the national monuments, we had tried to reconcile the positions of the conservationist House and the development-sympathetic Senate. The result was an all-night meeting at which we thought we had hammered out a compromise.

Memorable performances were delivered by a laid-back Mo Udall and a fiery Ted Stevens. Stevens would use temper as a weapon, sputtering that proposed boundaries of a park or wildlife refuge were totally unacceptable. On this issue or that, Stevens would say he was prepared to leave the table. Udall would smile, wait for the outburst to end, and then say, "Ted, how 'bout this?" He would make some cosmetic concession, and we would go on.

We had a deal, or so we thought. Nobody, however, anticipated the actions of Alaska's lightly regarded, show-horse junior senator, Mike Gravel. He signed off on the agreement one day, but twenty-four hours later denounced it and threatened a filibuster if the lands proposal reached the Senate floor. We lost the chance to settle the battle of Alaska in 1978.

Two years later, it was down to the last chance. We were back in the same place, with separate House and Senate bills and no chance of a compromise. But Reagan was a month away from taking office. We had to make a strategic decision.

The forces campaigning for parks and wildlife refuges could swallow the Senate bill, with its complications and compromises, or watch four years of work go down the tubes. All we had to do, in a lame-duck session of Congress, was get the House to go along with the Senate legislation.

The environmental groups were initially hostile. I actually had to listen to the idiotic argument that they could get a better Alaska package out of Reagan and Watt. Cooler heads quickly prevailed, however. For perhaps the only time in the movement's history, environmental leaders had to look at each other and say,

"This is all we can get." It proved the old adage that there's nothing like a hanging in the morning to focus the mind. Even though we were creating tomorrow's controversies, a 103-million-acre plan—amounting to more than 25 percent of Alaska—was a helluva lot better than nothing.

As part of the deal, we ended up protecting almost all of Admiralty Island, and at eight million acres Gates of the Arctic National Park is one of the world's largest protected areas. Some people never forgot or forgave us. Fourteen years after the Alaska Lands Act became law, Representative Don Young would grumble to an interviewer, "Jimmy Carter and Cecil Andrus locked up Alaska." In my ears, those were words of tribute.

I STOOD IN THE EAST ROOM THAT MORNING IN 1980, waiting for Carter to arrive to sign the lands act, with a lot of memories of people and places flashing across my mind. Soon my U-Haul would be loaded, and I'd be headed back to Idaho. A culminating achievement would send me home.

I thought of my dad, who taught me to fish and schooled me in the first and most essential lesson about both fishing and conservation: If you mess up a stream, there won't be any more fish. Anger over watching places get messed up became one of my strongest motivating factors in politics.

My thoughts flashed forward to the 1960s, when I was finding my voice in the Idaho Legislature. The U.S. Forest Service allowed logging on steep slopes above the south fork of the Salmon River. We had a heavy, early winter snowpack, followed by warm rains. With no vegetation to hold back the water, streams ran chocolate brown, and the resulting floods swept away millions of salmon eggs and ruined one of Idaho's choicest salmon runs.

The arguments of Alaska's mining executives dissolved into another memory. Miners in Idaho's Silver Valley had helped elect me governor. Soon after I took office, I found that children in the valley were suffering from lead poisoning. The south fork of the Coeur d'Alene River ran reddish brown as it flowed into a lake that is a scenic and recreational gem of my state. The mines would close, jobs would vanish, but a billion-dollar Superfund cleanup job would remain.

I thought, finally, of the White Cloud Mountains, where the American Smelting and Refining Company wanted to put a giant open-pit mine. "They're not going to tear down the mountains; they're going to dig a hole," my predecessor, Governor Don Samuelson, declared.

The hole was going to be gouged out of the heart of our state, an area with fifty-four backcountry fishing lakes and an 11,824-foot mountain, Castle Peak, that is the mother of all Idaho landmarks. Frog Lake, at its base, was to become a giant tailing pond.

I beat Don Samuelson, aided by two hundred thousand Idahoans who carried a hunting or fishing license, and stopped the rape of the White Clouds. The range became part of the six-hundred-thousand-acre Sawtooth National Recreation Area. As governor, one of my first acts was to send packing another mining outfit that wanted to exploit a lead and zinc deposit just north of Idaho's Craters of the Moon National Monument. The company needed to build a smelter and did not want to install scrubbers to prevent air pollution. "Fine, you can be on your way," I told them. The ore body would have had a duration of only four years, creating transitory jobs in exchange for permanent environmental damage.

The experiences in Idaho had prepared me for the greatest conservation battle of all, Alaska. After watching so many mistakes, here was the opportunity to do things right. And the chance to work on it was given to me by Jimmy Carter.

Carter had been elected governor of Georgia the same year that I upset Samuelson. Governors conferences gave us the chance to meet, become friends, and grow comfortable dealing with each other. In 1974, I won reelection while he left the Georgia statehouse to embark on what many thought was a quixotic quest for the White House. I had come to recognize the determination in those blue eyes and did not chuckle when the "unknown former Georgia governor" began to tour Iowa and New Hampshire saying, "My name is Jimmy Carter and I'm running for president."

I was still in the statehouse in 1976 when voters sent Carter to the White House. I wasn't planning to go anywhere when, without warning, a summons came to serve in his cabinet. The call came at 6 P.M., Boise time, from Carter's transition team. Carter wanted to meet with me at 8 A.M. the next day in Plains, Georgia. Presidents and presidents-elect have a way of summoning people across great distances with the confidence that somehow they'll be there in a flash.

I slept not a wink that night, flying from Boise to Seattle and then taking the Northwest red-eye to Atlanta. We rented a Cessna 172 and bumped down on a two-thousand-foot-long grass airstrip in Plains. Haggard, dirty, and bleary-eyed, I looked up at a terrifying sight: Sam Donaldson and Helen Thomas were charging across the grass toward my plane. Was there still time to fly back to Boise?

The picture was so very different four years later. Excitement enveloped Reagan, and Carter was seemingly forgotten by those questing for access to the man who would succeed him. One newspaper ran a cartoon showing Carter's bust sitting between dusty statues of Millard Fillmore and James Buchanan.

ONE MORE QUESTION THAT FLASHED ACROSS MY MIND in the East Room that day: Was there any way I could repay Carter for his faith in me and support for the Alaska Lands Act? I had taken the president on a raft trip down the middle fork of Idaho's Salmon River and taught him how to fly-fish for cutthroat trout. Somehow it didn't seem like enough.

The question lingers eighteen years later. What I'd really like to do, sometime before each of us is too long in the tooth, is take Jimmy Carter to one of the places he protected in Alaska: the long, deep-blue Walker Lake in the middle of the Brooks Range. The lake was my base camp for two nights when I took federal officials and journalists on a 1978 tour of proposed parklands.

Walker Lake is one of the finest fishing spots on earth. I spent hours on the lake with my fly rod, casting well past midnight on one of those summer evenings in the far north when there is perpetual light. The arctic grayling rose to the fly and fought me with skill and verve. I caught and released more than a dozen of the fish.

A beer would have been nice after such rewarding labors, and therein lies the secret of Walker Lake. An Alaska outdoor writer, Craig Medred, had been sent out by rowboat to lower a burlap bag filled with beer to the bottom of the lake, with a rope and float to mark its location for retrieval. He accidentally let go of the rope, sending our supply of beer to an icy resting place.

I'd love to go back to Walker Lake with Jimmy Carter in tow. We could bring Medred along, give him a wet suit, and make him dive for the lost beer. Since leaving office, Carter has taken up fly-fishing with a vengeance and with engineering precision. He spends hours tying flies.

If ever I get my former boss to the shores of Walker Lake, I've debated what to say to him. But circumstances would probably dictate my words: "Goddamit, Mr. President, get your waders on and let's show some of those flies to the fish."

Chapter 5

RIVER OF
NO RETURN

M Y FATHER'S FORMAL EDUCATION stopped at the eighth grade, but he knew how to teach the fundamentals of Northwest history to his children. He took me, as a little boy, to watch Indian fishermen at Celilo Falls on the Columbia River. The scene was much as Lewis and Clark described it early in the nineteenth century. Tiny figures perched on frail platforms above churning, swirling, surging green waters. The river dropped thirty-eight feet at the falls, the culmination of its passage through the Cascade Range.

The Indians used long poles with nets attached at the end. They would stand, still as statues, intently peering into the river's eddies and whitecaps. The wait would end with sudden, swift jabs into the water in hopes of scooping up salmon that were leaping upstream. Before the coming of the white man, multiple falls and rapids at The Dalles made this area North America's premier gathering place for aboriginal peoples. When Lewis and Clark passed this way in 1805, they estimated that at least five tons of salmon were drying on scaffolds near the Columbia River cataracts. Meriwether Lewis was the first to write about the salmon in the Columbia River: "The multitudes of this fish are almost inconceivable. The water is so clear that they can readily be seen at the depth of 15 or 20 feet."

Celilo Falls is no more. In 1954, the cascades were forever inundated when the Army Corps of Engineers built The Dalles Dam. The sites of Indian encampments are now home to an aluminum smelter.

I am a product of both the old and new economies of the Pacific Northwest. Still-plentiful salmon were a vital part of the family diet of an Oregon boy growing up in Hood River during the Great Depression. Later, when I was a young husband and mill manager in Orofino, Idaho, fishing became my time for respite and thinking.

In the early 1980s, however, I was a media spokesman for the

Northwest aluminum industry as it struggled to hold on to public acceptance and sustain the high requirements for electricity and low power rates needed for its survival. Some would say it's a contradiction to care about fish while working for the energy-gobbling makers of aluminum. Bullpucky! Hundreds of the Northwest's aluminum workers are also dedicated fishermen. The West is a place where people work to live. And, to a fisherman, sport is one of life's essential experiences—recreation that renews life.

There's a bigger point to make here, however, one debunking old myths from the right side of the political spectrum about a choice of "power versus fish" or "jobs versus the environment." Such stuff has long been peddled by propagandists of what was alleged to be progress.

The issue really involves fish and the cost of electricity. The Bonneville Power Administration, which markets power in the Northwest, has made a big issue about its being required to spend millions of dollars to restore salmon runs. But the bureaucrats in Portland say little about other costs with which they have burdened the ratepayers. Through Bonneville's wholesale rates, the Pacific Northwest is still paying for two abandoned, partially built Washington Public Power Supply System nuclear plants and one completed WPPSS reactor that stands as a white elephant in the eastern Washington desert. Meanwhile, the federal power agency is housed in a fancy new Portland headquarters. I think the last guy to build such an edifice was Benito Mussolini. The agency's administrative costs have ballooned in recent years—although cutbacks have lately been forced on it—and its consultants' budget has long been out of control. Still, the agency claims that fish are a prime threat to our region's low electrical rates. It's a classic application of a dictum coined by *New York Times* columnist Tom Wicker: Hell hath no fury like a bureaucracy defending itself.

I am convinced, from more than twenty-five years of dealing with these issues, that it was possible—and *is* possible—for the Pacific Northwest to have both the hydropower and industry symbolized by the smelter at The Dalles, and the mighty salmon runs so important to the region's identity, history, and economy. All that is needed is a modest sense of balance and use of intelligence by the Army Corps of Engineers, the Bonneville Power Administration, and the interests that have benefited from transformation of the Columbia River system.

As early as 1938, Oregon journalist and future senator Dick Neuberger wrote of the Northwest: "Prevalent throughout the principal salmon-producing region of the world today is the almost unshakable opinion that within a few years the fighting fish with the flaky pink flesh will be one and the same with the dodo bird: extinct."

It has taken sixty long years for Neuberger's prophecy to approach reality. Salmon runs have struggled to survive, but have been depleted in a Columbia River transformed into an almost unbroken series of reservoirs. Even above the manmade lakes, in the unspoiled spawning habitat of the wonderful, wild-running Salmon River of my home state, salmon verge on extinction. There are just too many dams downstream.

The disappearance of salmon disturbs me for a variety of reasons. I'm aware that the Snake and Salmon Rivers were once the spawning destination for a third of the salmon and steelhead in the Columbia River system. An incredible 2.5 million wild chinook once inhabited Idaho's greatest river system. A few thousand return now.

As an Idaho fisherman, I'm angry that my state has not been able to hold a sportfishing season on salmon for twenty years. I have a sense of legacy. I want to pass on the best of the Northwest to my children and grandchildren. When I give the gift of a lifetime Idaho fishing license, I want my grandchild to be able to use it for his or her entire life. As a public official, I was offended by the lack of foresight whenever I visited dams and encountered fish bypass systems that simply didn't work. I was outraged at what seemed to be a deliberate disregard of potential consequences by the federal agencies that harnessed the Columbia River.

I have likened the loss of salmon to another great problem of the Northwest, radioactive garbage buried at the federal government's nuclear reservations in Washington and Idaho. The feds invested enormous resources at the front end, building great dams for power and pioneering reactor technology to make plutonium for nuclear weapons. Little thought went into the other end, providing for the fish and handling the radioactive byproducts. The same applies to the fish in our rivers. The people who created the problems did not deal with the aftereffects until the eleventh hour. By that time, we had endured the inevitable screwups and wasted dollars that result when agencies scramble to come up with band-aid solutions.

RESTORING SALMON BECAME AN OBSESSION DURING my last two terms as governor of Idaho. After years of ordering that an action be taken, or taking it, or maneuvering to make something happen, I found myself squeezed and frustrated. Salmon were disappearing, but I was up against bureaucracies that could not be moved to save them. When I finally left office in early 1995, a sympathetic state legislator named Jim Stoicheff said of me: "Everything he touches turns to gold." Sad to say, that wasn't the case with the cause I fought hardest and longest for, and cared about the most.

In an era when people talked of such radical measures as draining the Lake Powell reservoir behind Glen Canyon Dam to restore a free-flowing Colorado River, the state of Idaho put forward a modest proposal to bring back our salmon. I presented it to federal agencies managing the Columbia River system. I briefed Northwest governors. I took my case to the White House and Northwest lawmakers in Washington, D.C.

We did not propose to blow up or breach any dams. Instead, we wanted to lower the reservoirs behind four dams on the Snake River in eastern Washington for six or eight weeks each spring. The river would go back into a narrow channel, the velocity of water would increase, and juvenile salmon would be swept downstream to the Pacific Ocean. The fish would take a week or two to reach the ocean, instead of spending often-deadly months in reservoirs—or being trucked or barged around dams in an abysmally unsuccessful program begun by the Army Corps of Engineers in the 1970s. With our plan, the dams would be equipped with new screens and channels to allow for fish passage. We would make the Snake River work the way it used to.

In swimming upstream against federal bureaucracies, I sometimes felt like a salmon returning from the Pacific Ocean to confront the colossus of Grand Coulee Dam. The Idaho plan would have upset Bonneville's way of doing business. The agency liked to generate lots of kilowatts at those Snake River dams at the time of year when water is most needed for survival of fish. Where did the power go? It went to California. Low-cost hydroelectric kilowatts were gold to the Golden State, allowing its utilities to shut down coal-fired power plants in the Southwest.

In 1993, early in the Clinton administration, I tried to explain the salmon crisis and the Idaho plan to White House bigwigs including presidential aide Phil Lader and Council on Environmental Quality director Katie McGinty. They had no knowledge of Northwest salmon. They had no desire to disrupt the Northwest-Southwest power intertie. They sat politely and said little, having received me at 1600 Pennsylvania Avenue only because I was a senior Democratic governor. I was just as politely shown the door.

What these folks didn't understand was that the stakes in the Northwest's salmon crisis far surpassed the survival of fish. Salmon are an indicator species of whether our region can live up to its self-image as one of the least degraded corners of the North American continent. Timothy Egan, in his book *The Good Rain*, put it best: "The Northwest is anywhere a salmon can get to." And Meriwether Lewis was among the first to find that out. Shortly after crossing Lemhi Pass, he was served a piece of roasted salmon, which he devoured with "great relish. This was the first salmon I had seen and perfectly convinced me that we were on the waters of the Pacific Ocean."

The salmon that Lewis remarked on was hatched in the upper Salmon River of what is now Idaho. Even now, the upper Salmon River is a place less transformed by man than almost any other corner of America in the nearly two hundred years since Lewis and Clark passed by. A guest-ranch operator of my acquaintance, Jack Briggs, could sit out on his porch on warm summer evenings, light his pipe, and tell his clients how William Clark carved his initials on a nearby pine tree as he sought to find out whether the Salmon River was navigable.

"When we bought this place, I'd count 250 salmon in a season out in that creek," Briggs said shortly before he sold the ranch. "The last one I saw was two years ago. Nothing wrong with the spawning beds. All the country around here is wilderness or semiwilderness. It's the dams."

The dams. Not on the Salmon River. The river was once dammed near its headwaters, in 1911, to provide power for the Sunbeam Mine. In 1934, however, a party or parties unknown ran a dynamite-laden raft into Sunbeam Dam. The river again flowed freely and was repopulated by the salmon whose migration had been blocked. Hundreds of miles downstream, however, far below where the Salmon joins the Snake River, the fish must run a gauntlet of eight federal dams before they reach the Pacific Ocean at Astoria, Oregon.

The benefits of these dams are endlessly touted. The Northwest receives low-cost energy. The dams help heat Californians' hot tubs during spring and summer months. With a line of reservoirs on the lower Snake River, the Army Corps of Engineers was able to make Lewiston, Idaho, four hundred miles upstream from the Pacific, into a barge port for export of grain.

When the reservoir reached Lewiston in February 1975 and a running river became slack water, the Corps had also completed a death trap for millions of young salmon being carried by the current on their way to the Pacific. A journey that once took a week to ten days, in the spring runoff of a free-flowing river, now takes a month or longer in a dammed river. The eight large blocks of concrete cause the smolts to lose their bearings and fall prey to every type of critter from squawfish to seagulls. Most of them die trying to navigate the dams.

If you want to understand the consequences of the damming of the Snake River, visit Redfish Lake, high in Idaho's Sawtooth Mountains. The lake came by its name from the thousands of red-bodied, green-snouted sockeye salmon that once spawned in its clear, cool waters. These sockeye were remarkable fish, swimming nearly nine hundred miles upstream from the ocean, climbing more than 6,500 vertical feet, and not eating for most of the monthlong freshwater journey.

A total of 1,118 returning sockeye salmon were counted in 1963 at Ice Harbor Dam near the mouth of the Snake River. In the early 1990s, however, only one to four sockeye made it back to the lake each year. A weir below the lake, where biologists trap the fish to remove their eggs, became a kind of shrine to the imperiled species. Local folks staged candlelight vigils. Banners encouraged the sockeye: "Spawn 'Til You Drop" and "Spawn Your

Brains Out" were my favorite slogans. It may have been to no avail, however. Sixteen adult sockeye returned to Redfish Lake in 1987. By 1991, the total was down to four. In 1995, not a single sockeye was captured at the weir.

A $13 million hatchery sits not far from Redfish Lake. Its job is to remove eggs from returning salmon and raise their young, a job done with constantly improving technology. Downstream, however, about nine out of every ten chinook and sockeye smolts released by the Corps-built hatchery are killed going through the Corps' turbines and spillways.

The irony wasn't lost on Rick Alslager, who ran the hatchery during my second stint as governor. "We are gaining in technology to put fish down the river," he would explain, "but we can't keep up with what we are losing through the dams. If we are to do any good here, we've got to get our little fish to the ocean."

DEVELOPMENT OF THE COLUMBIA RIVER SYSTEM HAS been a story of gains flowing downstream, where most of the people live, and pains staying upstream. The harnessing of the river has meant flood control downstream: Never again will we see the likes of the inundation of Vanport, Oregon, near Portland, in 1948. In order to achieve this goal—and to store water for power generation—great valleys have been inundated upstream in Idaho, Montana, and British Columbia. In my state, the reservoir behind Dworshak Dam is fifty-four miles long at full pool.

Since World War II, the Northwest has produced a third of the nation's primary aluminum. Cheap power attracted the smelters and spurred industrialization in such places as Portland, Tacoma, Spokane, and Seattle. Still, only two of the region's seven smelters—at Mead, near Spokane, and in Columbia Falls, Montana—are located in upstream reaches of the Columbia River system.

There is also an upstream-downstream issue with salmon. Downstream, with only four dams to pass through, a fairly healthy fall chinook salmon run survives in the Hanford Reach of the Columbia, the lone undammed stretch of river between Bonneville Dam and the Canadian border. The National Marine Fisheries Service is pressing the local utilities that own dams on the mid-Columbia River to conclude a far-reaching agreement on river flow, passage of salmon through dams, and restoration of salmon habitat. The utilities have shown a welcome willingness to accommodate the fish.

Upstream, the story is different. The Salmon River in Idaho once produced about 30 percent of the Columbia River's spring chinook salmon and more than 40 percent of its summer chinook. Before it was submerged by Dworshak Dam, the north fork of the Clearwater River was one of the world's greatest habitats for steelhead. A total of 94,301 chinook salmon were counted at Ice Harbor Dam, just up the Snake River from its confluence with the Columbia, in 1962. Since then, runs that once numbered thousands of salmon now count just a few hundred fish. In 1995, fewer than a thousand spring and summer chinook made it back to upstream spawning beds. In 1991, when the fish was listed as an endangered species, there were about nine thousand chinook.

In the mid-1950s, at the time The Dalles Dam was built, anglers in Idaho caught about twenty thousand chinook salmon and between twelve thousand and thirty thousand steelhead each year. Twenty years later, as gates were closing on the Corps' dams on the lower Snake River, the chinook catch had dwindled to fifteen hundred fish. More steelhead than salmon were being caught, but the seagoing trout was suffering the same sort of decline. After 1975, charts on the chinook catch in Idaho begin to bear the same two words each year: "Season closed."

Downstream, gillnet fishermen were still operating at the mouth of the Columbia River. Charter boats were still running out of Ilwaco. Indians were still netting salmon along the river—for religious and ceremonial use, but also for restaurants in San Francisco.

When I was first elected governor, I told an assistant to find out if the state of Idaho could buy a surplus minesweeper. My dream was to go right down the Columbia and take out every fish net in the river. We found a minesweeper. The price tag was a hundred thousand dollars, but the cost of an engine retrofit put it out of my budget.

Would I have gone that far? Maybe. The sportsmen of Idaho were getting zero. I was one of 'em, and I was mad as hell. I'm still angry.

On a recent trip up the Clearwater River, I passed the spot near Lewiston where I became the first American governor to blow up a dam. I pushed the detonator that destroyed the only dam on the main stem of the Clearwater. It was a low reregulating dam, with a fish ladder, but an impediment nonetheless. On the same trip, I also drove by the place where Idaho's record steelhead, a thirty-pounder, was landed. It was taken in 1973, just as the dams were going in downstream on the Snake River.

Steelhead are still caught on the Clearwater, but the runs are starting to dwindle. The decline is slower—steelhead are a heartier fish than salmon—but the result will be the same. The decline of steelhead fishing in Idaho threatens what, in my view, is one of the premier outdoor experiences of the American West. It is an incredible thrill to hook, and then match wits with, a wild creature that weighs (usually) between eight and eighteen pounds and often has the fortitude and guile to free itself.

These experiences were in my thoughts as we spotted the riffle in the Clearwater, near Orofino's airport, where I caught my last salmon. I looked again at Black Rock and Bruce's Eddy and other places where I fished and picnicked as a young man raising a family in a small Northwest town. Folks used to travel a road up the north fork of the Clearwater to fish after a hard day's work. The road is no more, submerged beneath waters backed up by 717-foot-high Dworshak Dam, the last high dam to be built in the Northwest.

Of course, the Army Corps of Engineers promised mitigation for the miles of spawning habitat wiped out by its dam. They built the world's largest fish hatchery for steelhead at Orofino. But the hatchery has been besieged year after year by diseases.

Dworshak Dam was not necessary as a power or water storage project and was, in hindsight, a mistake. In the 1960s, as the state senator from Clearwater County, I had believed in all the propaganda of progress and had shortsightedly supported its construction—one of the few genuine regrets of my life in politics.

The Corps uses the dam for peaking power, electricity needed at times of maximum demand. Since the late 1980s, it's been drawing down the reservoir even at times when boaters and recreationists use it most. Heavy drawdowns have destroyed summer recreation on the reservoir. In steelhead season, anglers downstream must deal with river levels that rise and fall several feet in a day.

THE ARMY CORPS OF ENGINEERS BEGAN ITS WORK ON the Columbia River in a flush of New Deal idealism during the 1930s. It drew up a plan for Bonneville Dam with no provision for a fish bypass system. A cry arose that united the fisheries industry and Indian tribes in a single demand. As Dick Neuberger, Oregon's future U.S. senator, summed up opinion at the time, "The salmon must get up the river."

The Corps ended up spending $7 million—a handsome sum in the 1930s—on a system of fish ladders. People held their breath and the giant stairs seemed to work in getting migrating adult salmon sixty-five vertical feet up and over the dam. If the federal agency's original plan had prevailed, however, salmon and steelhead would have inhabited only the lower 145 miles of a river system that drains an area larger than France. The Corps wouldn't have let fish pass through the dam.

The fish ladders allowed salmon to get upstream. The fish had to climb 774 steps at various dams on the Snake and Salmon Rivers. In the 1930s, and for four decades afterward, however, no thought was given to the mortality rate of young salmon moving downstream. About 10 to 20 percent died at each dam.

Much of the upper river system was permanently closed off to salmon migration. Grand Coulee Dam, a U.S. Bureau of Reclamation project, was the greatest fish killer. Built without fish ladders, it cut off eleven hundred miles of habitat in the Columbia and its tributaries. Salmon once swam as far upstream in the Columbia River—into the trench between the Rocky and Purcell Mountains in British Columbia—as in the Snake River of Idaho. Thousands of upstream-bound sockeye salmon beat themselves to death against Grand Coulee's 343-foot-high face. Waters of its reservoir inundated Kettle Falls, the other great native gathering place on the river, where Indians had once dried up to six hundred thousand pounds of salmon each fall.

In my state, the Idaho Power Company built three dams in Hells Canyon during the late 1950s. The Federal Power Commission permit required the passage of salmon. The company promised it could be done. Since these are high dams, fish ladders were not possible. Instead, adult salmon were trapped and trucked above the dams; a net in Brownlee Reservoir captured the young fish migrating downstream, who were then given motorized transportation.

It didn't work. Idaho Power stopped trapping fish, paid for three hatcheries, and claimed that Snake River salmon had been "relocated" in the Salmon River. The U.S. Fish and Wildlife Service pegs the loss from those three dams at about a million fish. A big chunk of the Snake was forever closed off to salmon and steel-head, and fluctuating river levels in the wild part of Hells Canyon often left spawning beds high and dry.

Still, that loss pales in comparison to the damage caused by these eight Army Corps of Engineers dams downstream on the Snake and Columbia Rivers. They stand in the way of wild salmon, hatchery fish, and any other living creature trying to make it downstream.

Over the last six decades, the chief players on the river system have been electrical utilities, aluminum producers, irrigators, and—above all—two federal agencies: The Corps of Engineers builds the dams and oversees the power system; the Bonneville Power Administration sells electricity and protects its customers.

Initially with idealistic motives—"Your power is turning the darkness to dawn," sang Woody Guthrie in his brief stint as a troubadour for the BPA—Bonneville set about building a river economy of irrigated deserts, abundant cheap power, smelters, and barges moving grain. Natural creatures were expected to yield, adjust, or go away. If fish ladders saved salmon runs, fine. If not, progress had its price.

In 1968, for instance, the Corps of Engineers was preparing to dedicate John Day Dam on the Columbia River. The dam was finished, but its fish ladders were not yet operational. Vice President Hubert Humphrey was due to speak at dedication ceremonies. The Corps ordered the dam's gates to be closed: Ladders or no ladders, the dedication would go forward. As a result, thousands of migrating adult salmon died below the dam. The people who did this were not evil, just bound by the military-bureaucratic mind-set and blindly focused on their goals. When they thought of salmon, it was never in terms of adjusting or modifying plans—or simply not building something—but in terms of Rube Goldberg–style contraptions that would put things right.

In 1979, as interior secretary, I stood at Lower Granite Dam on the Snake River. It was time for a VIP briefing by the Army Corps of Engineers on the mitigation of spawning habitat flooded by the Corps' four dams downstream from Lewiston. My concern was not with the fish ladders, which worked for adult salmon, but with the cumulative effect of four dams on the smolts—young salmon and steelhead—headed downstream to the ocean.

With charts and graphs worthy of General H. Norman Schwarzkopf, the Corps colonels droned on with the statistics. A total of $50 million had been spent on fish passage at the four dams. A $220 million compensation plan was being put into place. I was given target figures on the fish that would be released from hatcheries. But there was no acknowledgment of the high mortality experienced once hatchery fish are released into the river. When the discussion turned to the problem of young salmon being killed as they passed through dams, the colonels detailed an elaborate plan called the Juvenile Fish Transportation Program. They would catch young salmon and steelhead at Little Goose and Lower Granite Dams, and truck and barge the fish more than three hundred miles downstream to a point below Bonneville Dam.

In the Corps' worldview, trucking and barging would eliminate the hazards of dam turbines and nitrogen supersaturation. (Fish, like humans, can get the bends after being submerged in deep water.) What they did not understand is that we do not entirely comprehend what signals fish absorb as they swim downstream that, three years later, allow them to return to a distant river home.

The charts, graphs, and maps failed to impress me. I bluntly voiced worries about disease, confusion, and vulnerability to predators among the fish being trucked around the dams. What I heard was, "That's a good question, Mr. Secretary."

I alternately cajoled and cussed out the Corps brass, trying to hammer into their skulls the importance of keeping their promises to maintain salmon in the Snake River. They didn't listen; they didn't have to, even when a cabinet secretary was talking. The Army Corps of Engineers has always seemed to me to have laws unto itself, being a largely autonomous agency of the U.S. Department of Defense. While I might have had President Carter's ear as secretary of the interior, I did not have the horsepower to overcome these colonels.

I wish to this day that, on that afternoon at the dam in 1979, I would have instructed the U.S. Fish and Wildlife Service to start hammering on endangered species listings. Perhaps the Corps could have been forced to change its policies.

Meanwhile, the salmon runs declined year after year. As governor in the 1980s and 1990s, I could not budge these bland, bureaucratic though pleasant people who were absolutely set on doing things their own way. In 1994, as in 1979, I was still asking why their contraptions didn't work. The colonels had the same answer, though recognizing my new title: "That's a good question, governor."

IN 1980, AN OLD POLITICAL ADVERSARY OF MINE, Representative John Dingell of Michigan, tried to give migrating fish a little help in the law. When Congress passed the Northwest Power Act, setting a framework for the region's energy future, it was Dingell who insisted that fish production be defined as a "co-equal partner" with energy generation on the Columbia River system. The law set out, as its goal, "to protect, mitigate, and enhance" salmon and steelhead populations.

A new policy-making body, the Northwest Power Planning Council, was set up to direct energy policy and the restoration of salmon in streams of the Columbia River system. The governors of Washington, Oregon, Idaho, and Montana were each given two appointments to the council. At last, upstream states seemed to have some clout. But the power council was based downstream in Portland, close by the offices of the Corps and Bonneville Power Administration, and cheek-to-jowl with the powerful lobbies defending the status quo on the river.

The council, chaired by ex-Washington Governor Dan Evans, an outdoorsman and one of the finest public servants with whom I ever worked, set an objective of doubling salmon and steelhead runs from 2.5 million fish to 5 million fish. (The Columbia River once saw 16 million salmon and steelhead migrate back upstream each year.)

It was a noble goal. In pursuing it, however, the council followed the path of least resistance and sought the most ample source of water. The first big project was to resurrect the salmon runs of Washington's Yakima River, which had been destroyed by irrigation early in this century. The fish had an eloquent witness in future U.S. Supreme Court Justice William O. Douglas, who had explored the upper reaches of the river as a boy.

Workable ladders were put on irrigation dams, and weirs were erected on canals to keep salmon from swimming into farm fields. The Yakima River project was given a boost when, at the behest of the Yakama Indian Nation, a U.S. District Court judge set down minimum river-flow levels that the Bureau of Reclamation had to follow.

The council also set out to boost the so-called "water budget"—informally known as the fish flush—down the main stem of the Columbia River. The flush is a procedure under which a fixed amount of water is released down the river at peak times of juvenile salmon migration. Because the technique moves smolts more quickly down the river, fewer fall victim to predators. Biologists are actually able to spot concentrations of smolts on radar, and get to trigger the water release.

The flush wasn't nearly enough. The council seemed to

studiously ignore the Snake River, where salmon runs were in a crisis state. Our river was given a water budget, but it was much smaller than that of the Columbia.

I can't say the power council was neutered, because I don't believe it ever had any balls to begin with. The panel experienced a brief springtime of influence when Evans was chairman. But he was soon named to a U.S. Senate vacancy. The power council became lost in meetings, process, and the massive generation of paperwork. The downstream power interests had the time and resources to keep up with and influence its decisions.

Sad to say, even though I named members of the outfit, the power council wasn't about to upset the power managers of the Columbia River system. Indeed, the Corps of Engineers and Bonneville Power Administration never formally recognized the council's authority. The message was clear: If the council ordered these agencies to take any action that really disturbed business as usual on the river, they were prepared to ignore the panel.

My fondest hope is that the fish flush, along with other measures, will restore a healthy run of sockeye salmon to places like Lake Wenatchee in the Washington Cascades. But these fish live off the main Columbia River. Careful management of that river doesn't do a damned thing to bring sockeye back to Redfish Lake, at the headwaters of the Salmon River in the Sawtooth Mountains of Idaho. Ours was the river shortchanged, along with the Snake River, into which it flows.

IN POLITICS, UNFORTUNATELY, THERE IS A TENDENCY to deal with crises of the moment and put off all other problems. An unexpected shock is usually required as a stimulus to action. In this respect, I'm again reminded of the old adage that there's nothing like a hanging in the morning to focus the mind.

The Northwest's hanging came in 1989, a near-drought year that followed three other years in which spring runoff in the region's rivers was below average. The numbers of returning salmon, particularly in the Snake River, dwindled into the hundreds. It was time to demand action, so I put forward the Idaho plan to draw down the reservoirs. But immediately there was resistance from entrenched interests, like port districts, that lived off river development. There were howls that transport of grain on barges out of Lewiston would be disrupted for two months a year and that some irrigators' pumps would be left high and dry for a spell.

We asked that the Corps of Engineers make the river more fish-friendly for what few salmon there were by installing bypass screens at its dams immediately, particularly at McNary and John Day Dams on the Columbia River. The screens are designed to keep young salmon from being sucked into the turbines, and to lead them toward channels that will guide them around the dams. The technology is, admittedly, expensive and much more tricky than fish ladders carrying adult salmon upstream. Still, the need for this measure was urgent. Barging and trucking of salmon—Army Corps of Engineers claims to the contrary—was not working. Each dam could kill up to 20 percent of the smolts that passed through it. If you factor in eight dams, you see why fish runs on the Snake and Salmon Rivers were rapidly sliding toward extinction.

It seemed, at the turn of the decade, that there was hope. The power council was split on what to do, and proposed much less drawdown on the Snake River. At that point, a more powerful player—Senator Mark Hatfield of Oregon—moved in. In June 1990, Hatfield convened a "salmon summit" of all the players on the Columbia. He was visibly angry at the Corps for dragging its feet on screens at the dams, telling the colonels: "I'm really bothered that we've had to push these bypasses on you."

The summit seemed to produce results. We won agreement for reservoir releases on the Snake River to provide a limited increase in flow. The power council proposed higher water budgets for both the Columbia and Snake Rivers—and agreed to test my idea of faster river flows through one three-month period on the Snake River. The reservoir level above Lower Granite Dam was lowered by thirty-seven feet in the spring of 1992.

The test was, however, a one-shot deal. In the years since, rulers of the river have shown just how tenaciously bureaucracies can defend themselves. The Corps and Bonneville mounted an in-depth defense of the way they ran the river. They built a tissue curtain of exaggerations and falsehoods. Bonneville hinted darkly that "thousands of megawatts" of power production would be lost if we drew down the reservoirs. Jack Robertson, deputy BPA administrator, warned that "the region may be left with environmentally damaging alternatives—such as burning coal and oil—to produce electricity." The agency hinted that electrical bills would go up by 16 percent.

It was enough to bring tears to your eyes if you happened to be a crocodile. This is the same agency that championed the Washington Public Power Supply System's nuclear program, which tripled the electrical rates of some homeowners and left the region with abandoned reactors. The cries of alarm were a lie. During spring runoff, dams on the lower Snake River don't generate a single kilowatt of energy that is needed in the Northwest. We ship the equivalent off to California to heat the hot tubs and hair-dryers of the Southland and to light the rides at Disneyland. Overall, those Snake River dams generate just 4.1 percent of the region's power.

The irrigators and barge operators mobilized and went to see their members of Congress. The chambers of commerce in Lewiston and Clarkston ran newspaper ads showing dead fish in a dry reservoir. Opponents of change also raised the specter of dawn turning back to darkness along the Columbia and Snake Rivers. Senator Slade Gorton, a Washington state Republican, used fish as bogeymen. He fanned fears during a 1994 speech in Pasco, warning of the prospect of sagebrush-covered farms and ruined towns in irrigation-dependent eastern Washington. "It's hard for me to think restoration of a few salmon runs is worthwhile if it means a thirty-foot drop in reservoir levels and productive farmland returning to desert," Gorton said.

Gorton is a smart fellow, surely smart enough to know that irrigation losses can be mitigated by lowering the intake pipes that take water out of the river.

The Corps of Engineers, in a delay tactic worthy of the Red Army in World War II, hinted that it might need to ask Congress for reauthorization of the dams if it were forced to lower the reservoirs behind them. The Corps also warned it would cost $1.3 billion to $4.9 billion to retrofit the dams so young salmon could pass downstream. The money figures were bogus. We had a study done that figured it would cost $637 million to retrofit dams for fish passage and lower irrigation intakes. Amortized over ten years, these effective measures would have cost less than the hatcheries and barging programs that had failed to work.

I marveled, however, at the tactics of the business-as-usual crowd. A make-believe vision of dusty ghost towns was created to shield the reality that adjustments could be made. The bureaucrats and utility executives ballooned the price tag of measures they did not want to take, just as they deliberately minimized cost estimates for projects like the WPPSS nuclear plants and posh Bonneville headquarters.

The Corps itself had studied the power issue. It pegged the loss at only 150 megawatts of power generation if Snake River reservoirs were drawn down. Its report concluded: "Under most conditions, we have more than enough capacity to satisfy Northwest needs."

Economists from the University of Idaho, Washington State University, and Oregon State University took a look at predictions of catastrophe for traffic on the Snake River. They found that only 5.4 percent of wheat shipped from Portland is barged down the river from Lewiston during the proposed drawdown period. "We conclude that shippers who presently depend on the lower Snake ports are likely to be very creative in modifying the time and mode of their shipments in response to any drawdown of the river," they found.

The objectives behind all the dire warnings by the Columbia River's rulers weren't hard to fathom. Ed Chaney, an Idaho resident who has devoted three decades of his life to saving salmon, put it thusly: "It's their standard operating procedure. You promise the rubes anything to build what you want to build. Then you don't deliver. If you screw things up too much, you declare the price is too high to fix it."

As Republicans took control of Congress in 1995, Senator Gorton began to talk more boldly of capping the money spent on salmon and allowing certain runs to go extinct. He didn't say where, but the finger of fate seemed pointed at the Snake River.

I watched other disturbing signs. The Republican Congress killed a test drawdown of the reservoir behind John Day Dam. Unwilling to upset the status quo, the National Marine Fisheries Service allowed nearly 80 percent of the Snake River's salmon smolts to be barged. I've tried to hold my tongue, often painfully, about motives of opponents. In this case, the objective seems painfully obvious. The people who run the Columbia River are playing for time. They are counting on delay to eliminate the problem by eliminating the salmon runs of the Snake and Salmon Rivers. They are in a race, not only with time but with evidence and public opinion and the law.

A recent study, commissioned by the Army Corps of Engineers, went further than the drawdowns and modifications to dams that I championed. The best way to avoid extinction of salmon, it suggested, would be to breach the four lower Snake River dams and restore the natural flow of the river. Breaching means permanently restoring the natural flow of a dammed river. It would be accomplished by removing the earth berms on both sides of each dam. The river would flow around the concrete barriers, which would be left in place in case someday the dams were needed again. The *Idaho Statesman* newspaper, hardly a radical voice in the Northwest, has endorsed breaching the dams.

It is increasingly apparent that lights won't flicker out if reservoirs are lowered, or even if the dams are breached. The four dams are not essential to a region presently awash with power-generating capacity. By delaying action on such alternatives as drawdowns, however, the players on the river are gambling the future of a great resource and quite likely making the Northwest a loser.

We lose a priceless part of our natural and cultural heritage, and a not inconsiderable economic asset, if salmon runs are allowed to go extinct. My state would suffer the most harm. A headline on a recent Associated Press story put it best: "Idaho Has Habitat, Needs Salmon."

The public seems to recognize the loss, and is of a mind to prevent it. Idahoans are among the nation's most conservative folk, but a recent statewide poll showed that about half the state's citizens would support removing the four lower Snake River dams. If the irrigators in the upper Snake River are ever asked to give more water to sustain questionable Army Corps of Engineers policies, I can guarantee you they will link arms with downstream sportsmen. Support for breaching the dams will rise to 70 percent.

Some people can't read the tea leaves, though. In her 1994 campaign, Idaho's intellectually challenged Representative Helen Chenoweth wondered why salmon can be considered an endangered species when you can buy canned salmon at Albertson's.

What obtuseness, what stupidity. As a young man in

Orofino, I went to the Clearwater River, not a market. A friend once quoted to me from Rudyard Kipling, who delivered the ultimate accolade to fishing for chinook salmon in the Columbia River: "I have lived! The American continent may now sink under the sea, for I have taken the best it yields and the best was neither money nor love nor real estate."

He wasn't talking about a trip to the supermarket.

WHEN LAST I LOOKED, THE ENDANGERED SPECIES ACT was still on the books. So was the 1855 Treaty of Walla Walla in which Isaac Stevens, the first governor of Washington Territory, spoke on behalf of the U.S. government and assured tribes that their fishing grounds would be forever protected.

It doesn't take a lawyer to see how the 1973 species act could be deployed to save salmon. Each major river system on the Northwest coast—and each major tributary in the Columbia-Snake River system—produces a genetically distinct run of salmon. Hence, there are hundreds of runs. According to the American Fisheries Society, a total of 214 of them face extinction. Several species, like coho salmon in the Snake River, are already extinct.

As long ago as 1979, the National Marine Fisheries Service toyed with trying to protect Columbia River salmon under the Endangered Species Act. I should have had the U.S. Fish and Wildlife Service join them, then and there. But the Carter administration was persuaded to hold off by prospects of a Northwest Power Act that would fix the problem.

As salmon disappear from rivers, the Northwest's Indian tribes are not inclined to such patience. In 1990 the Shoshone-Bannock Tribe petitioned the fisheries service to list the Snake River sockeye as endangered. Two months later, a coalition of environmental and outdoors groups petitioned for a similar listing of spring, summer, and fall chinook on the Snake River. The National Marine Fisheries Service responded by listing the Snake River sockeye as endangered—it's obvious when only one or two fish come back up the river—and declaring the chinook salmon to be threatened. The designation was temporarily upgraded to endangered in 1994.

Environmentalists have successfully used the Endangered Species Act to bring one foot-dragging federal agency before the bench. In the early 1990s, U.S. District Judge William L. Dwyer shut down timber sales in the coastal forests of the Northwest because of the U.S. Forest Service's "deliberate and systematic refusal" to draw up a viable plan for survival of the northern spotted owl. Dwyer's ruling should be required reading in the Bonneville Power Administration's notoriously know-it-all legal department. So should subsequent federal court rulings that salmon recovery plans drawn up by the Northwest Power Planning Council are wholly inadequate.

In the most ominous rumbling felt in Portland since Mount St. Helens was getting ready to blow, the U.S. Ninth Circuit Court of Appeals said of the four-state panel: "Rather than asserting its role as a regional leader, the Council has assumed the role of consensus builder, sometimes sacrificing the act's fish and wildlife goals for what is, in essence, the lowest common denominator acceptable to the power interests."

I would have put it in an unlawyerly fashion: They haven't helped the fish one goddamned bit.

What will the courts do if an enforcement suit is brought the next time the Northwest has a dry year in which power managers won't provide river flows needed for salmon survival? We could end up with a federal judge running the Columbia River system. The Bonneville Power Administration and Corps of Engineers would learn, quickly, that judges don't recognize agencies as laws unto themselves.

The judge could order that Snake River reservoirs be lowered for a much longer period than my proposal that caused yelping by irrigators and Lewiston-area port districts. A water release order from the bench could actually make the BPA's Chicken Little forecasts of potential power losses, and the Corps' warnings of costs, come true.

Rough justice perhaps, but I don't want it to happen. The Northwest has a history of visionary mediator-leaders, like Henry Jackson, Warren Magnuson, Frank Church, and Tom Foley, who came up with homegrown solutions to the region's problems. They are the reason why the Southwest never succeeded in grabbing our water, and why California has so much less say over the Columbia than over the Colorado River.

Our great fish runs, which awed Lewis and Clark in 1805 and later awed this Oregon schoolboy, have been sold down the river to business-as-usual. But it's not a case of permanent loss that must be accepted. The status quo on the Columbia-Snake River system is no longer sustainable. The hydropower system managers will be forced to confront the same choice given to many endangered species: Adapt or perish.

Chapter 6

BIRDS OF PREY AND OTHER PREDATORS

A N HOUR OUT OF BOISE, THE CANYON of the Snake River is a wild, windy escarpment with fast-moving clouds creating ever-changing shadow patterns, and sunsets making for a mosaic of colors. I stood on the canyon rim, a breeze in my face, as a retired Bureau of Land Management guide named Morley Nelson flushed a China pheasant into the air. I heard a whooshing sound! A peregrine falcon came out of the sky at nearly a hundred miles an hour. The falcon killed the pheasant in a millisecond, retracting one foot while extending the other to break the neck of its prey.

Cliffs along both sides of the river are home to the greatest density of nesting raptors in North America, the predatory birds including several species of hawks, golden eagles, falcons, and owls. That day with Morley Nelson, twenty-five years ago, taught me two key requirements of endangered species in the American West: They need habitat in which to breed and a steady food supply. The cliffs of the river provide a wonderfully secure place where hawks can take off hunting with assurance that the "kids" are safe in the nest. As for food, the fields outside of Boise abound with Townsend ground squirrels and black-tailed jackrabbits, tasty meals that hawks or falcons can carry for miles to the mouths they must feed.

If Idaho wanted to keep its noble raptors, I learned, we also had to preserve the humble ground squirrels. The food chain could not be broken, nor could the birds go someplace else and change their diet. Thus, habitat was the key issue in what would become a decade-long struggle to create a Birds of Prey Natural Area along the Snake River. We had to keep grasslands from going under the plow in order to assure hunting grounds for peregrine and prairie falcons. The land behind the river, much of which had been converted to agriculture, was their dining room.

Ultimately, the natural area spanned the river for eighty-one miles. As one of my last acts as secretary of the interior, I withdrew nearly half a million acres of land from development in order to guarantee the birds a food supply. It wasn't a lockup. Existing uses such as grazing, hunting, fishing, and National Guard training were allowed to continue. But the ground was not plowed up. One of the first things James Watt tried to do when he took over the Interior Department in 1981 was to overturn the birds of prey order. He failed.

The West has experienced a furious debate in recent years over how to preserve and restore species that the federal government once paid to have shot or poisoned. It is a debate, unfortunately, that has gravitated toward extreme positions and those absolutists who seek television exposure and see no compromise.

In one camp are the radical preservationists who would close off vast areas to human activity, and bring species back to habitats in which they can no longer survive. The other camp is represented by the rape-ruin-and-run boys (and girls) who would blow loopholes into environmental laws through which they could drive cement mixers and pave over wetlands.

Thankfully, our birds of prey project didn't become a test of strength for these warring, predatory camps. In the Snake River canyon, we took a look at uses of the falcons' dining room. Agricultural developers wanted to open additional acres closer to the rim of the canyon. An old political foe, Vern Ravenscroft—the only Idaho politician to lose gubernatorial primaries in both parties—was a booster of putting more land under the plow. He probably saw an issue that could separate me from the statehouse.

I was able to take an economic argument to those already tilling fields near the canyon. It would be to their benefit not to have additional land under irrigation. Not only would it mean competition, but pumping up more water from the Snake River would also involve enormous cost. Existing agriculture would not be harmed by creation of a sanctuary for eagles, hawks, and falcons. It would, in fact, be spared costly subsidized competition.

Nor would private inholdings be disturbed.

The Birds of Prey Natural Area eventually won acceptance as both a right action and a wise one. I ran for governor again in 1986 and Republicans tried to use the "lockup" against me. They quickly found the issue a nonstarter.

Whatever the radicals preach, peace and logic can win out. I winced not long ago when Sierra Club board member David Brower, a towering ego of American environmentalism, admonished followers to be wary of negotiating resolutions to environmental disputes at a local level. He seemed to argue that saving the earth precludes reasonable settlements between its users.

At the other extreme, I get embarrassed for my state whenever Helen Chenoweth utters some mindless remark about black helicopters carrying United Nations troops, or white males being the earth's real endangered species. Or when then-Senator Steve Symms said that Alaska has plenty of grizzly bears and all the rest would make excellent rugs.

While Brower may not admit it, we have seen remarkable progress and evolution of attitudes—at least within the United States. Early in this century, for instance, the National Park Service set out to eradicate wolves from Yellowstone National Park. In the winter of 1995, however, America's TV viewers saw Interior Secretary Bruce Babbitt helping lug a caged wolf into an enclosure near Mammoth Hot Springs. The wolf was being reintroduced to America's first national park. Shortly thereafter, the first of thirty wolves were released in Idaho's Frank Church–River of No Return Wilderness Area. The wolves are going great guns in Yellowstone; they've also prospered in Idaho, except for those that come out of the wilderness and under the gun.

The West's predatory birds, even America's national symbol, were once thought of as pests to be hunted and poisoned. Until the late 1950s, a bounty was paid on bald eagles in Alaska. Nowadays, the state of Alaska plays host to thousands of bald eagles (and hundreds of eagle watchers) each winter in the Chilkat River valley east of Glacier Bay National Park.

Few actions in my career have generated as much attention, public excitement, and personal satisfaction as creation of the Birds of Prey Natural Area. I was on the receiving end of supportive letters from schoolchildren and angry resolutions from farm organizations. Robert Redford, a raptor fan, floated the river and later returned as featured speaker at the fund-raising dinner when I was running for reelection as governor.

It was grand to have Redford raising money, but the handsome devil also had to send an autographed picture to my wife. She used Bob's visage to decorate a rolltop desk in our bedroom. The picture mysteriously toppled over two days in a row, and then somehow fell into a wastebasket. It was, suggested a suspicious Carol, "an inside job."

If Redford heard about some of the stands I've taken at present, he might be tempted to get the picture back. Take the grizzly bear, for example. The Interior Department is bent on returning *Ursus horribilis* to the Bitterroot Mountains on the Idaho-Montana border.

I'm a conservationist—I've even been called a tree hugger—but I dissent. The feds are running in the face of what Morley Nelson drilled into me more than a quarter-century ago on that canyon rim outside of Boise. The grizzlies and wolves need food. Without a natural supply, they will leave the wilderness and come into conflict with man. At one time, the country north of the Salmon River in what is now the Selway-Bitterroot Wilderness Area had a population of grizzlies. And that was when the Salmon River had a population of salmon. The bears had a plentiful diet of fish and berries.

How would the grizzlies make it today, when there are a few hundred salmon compared to four hundred thousand fish as recently as the 1950s? They would have to take food away from black bears. Grizzly bears (and wolves) will chase a cougar away from her kill. Or they will come down from the mountains and raid ranches for cattle and sheep.

Mother Nature is a smart lady. With a little help from man—for instance, prohibitions on hunting when numbers are low, and protection of migration corridors—she will do her thing. Humans bent on restoration of species will be making a mistake if they act with the same heavy hand as the exterminators did early in this century.

Take the wolf. Since being tracked and shot and poisoned early in the twentieth century, *Canis lupus* has been staging a quiet repopulation of parts of its former stomping grounds. Wolves have moved down out of the Flathead River valley in western Montana, at least as far as Missoula, and biologists believe some have already migrated into northern Idaho.

In Washington, a den of wolves has been found at the base of Mount Hozomeen in the Ross Lake National Recreation Area. *Canis lupus* has found an ideal migration corridor in the upper reaches of the Skagit River, which rises in a Canadian wilderness and feeds into a fjordlike reservoir that begins on the U.S. border. Both sides of the 49th parallel are protected. A U.S. park ranger snapped a memorable picture of a wolf sauntering through a playfield in British Columbia's Skagit Valley Recreation Area.

The wolf is welcomed by many in Idaho. It has supportive constituencies in places like Missoula and Bozeman, in Sun Valley and Boise. The Greater Yellowstone Coalition is offering opportunities to go out and howl with the wolves that are culling the huge ungulate populations in the northeast part of Yellowstone Park.

As wolves were being reintroduced in the Salmon River country, I sat down in Grangeville for a talk with Tom Kovalicky, retired supervisor of the Nez Perce National Forest, which covers much of north-central Idaho between the Clearwater and Salmon

Rivers. Tom is one of the wisest federal land managers I know. Kovalicky is convinced there are still wolves in the wilderness of central Idaho. He claims to know where they live.

Kovalicky kept quiet about *Canis lupus* so as to protect the wolves from politics. He didn't want to have hordes of scientists stumbling over their habitat. Nor did he want noisy hearings with Earth Firsters and sheep ranchers howling at each other in parking lots. "They're a small group," he says of the wolves, "and they're doing just dandy down there." If the food supply increases, the wolf population will grow and expand its habitat.

This tread-quietly approach makes a great deal of sense. The highly publicized release of wolves in the Frank Church–River of No Return Wilderness may have stirred the hearts of urban conservationists, but it raised the ire of local ranchers. They felt left out of the decision-making as well as threatened. A wolf was shot dead by a rancher within a few weeks of their much-publicized reintroduction in the Salmon River country.

CONGRESS ENACTED THE ENDANGERED SPECIES ACT IN 1973 during my first term as governor of Idaho. I would spend much of the next two decades dealing with its consequences, at the Interior Department, and then back at the Idaho statehouse. The act is the least yielding of the nation's environmental laws. A division of the Interior Department, the U.S. Fish and Wildlife Service, is instructed to maintain a list of species that are endangered or threatened. Once an animal or bug or fish or plant is so listed, humans are not allowed to "harass, harm, pursue, hunt, shoot, wound, kill, trap, capture, or collect" it. The wildlife service has to list every species that qualifies.

The agencies of the United States government are instructed to carry out their programs so as to conserve species listed as threatened or endangered. "Conserve" is defined as meaning the use of "all methods and procedures which are necessary to bring listed species to the point of recovery."

The law allows no wiggle room. We found that out in the Carter administration: A cabinet colleague, Attorney General Griffin Bell, tried to persuade the U.S. Supreme Court that the thumb-size snail darter should not be allowed to block construction of Tennessee's Tellico Dam. The dam would destroy the darter's habitat. Bell even passed a darter up to the bench.

The little fish in a vial inspired a crucial question from Supreme Court Justice John Paul Stevens: "Mr. Attorney General, your exhibit makes me wonder. Does the government take the position that some endangered species are entitled to more protection than others?"

Bell argued yes. The court said no. The snail darter was, in the eyes of the law, every bit as important as the bald eagle.

As interior secretary, I had told the Fish and Wildlife Service to bust its behind and uncover some other population of snail darters. I did not want that little fish to have such a high profile. It threatened a reaction that would sweep away protection for eagles and grizzly bears and wolves. We did find snail darters. The species lived. While not neutering the Endangered Species Act, political clout did push the Tellico project to completion.

Darter or no darter, Tellico Dam was a lousy project. It inundated Indian burial grounds, and the reservoir took more land out of agriculture than stood to be put into irrigation. Opponents raised economic objections, only to be overwhelmed by such powerful political advocates as Senator Howard Baker. Frustrated foes turned to the Endangered Species Act as a weapon of last resort. The law was being used as a weapon in a battle it had not been designed to fight.

The Endangered Species Act set down a policy to be followed by every agency of the government. Its authors should have realized, however, that federal agencies are themselves unique beasts subsisting on very different food chains. Within the Interior Department, we had a National Park Service of strong conservationist bent, with allies in the environmental movement, and a U.S. Bureau of Reclamation willing to pull out all the stops to defend its constituency of irrigators. We've also had interior secretaries of very different bents; witness myself and James Watt.

A successor of mine, Interior Secretary Manuel Lujan, picked up his *New York Times* one Sunday in 1990 and noticed a story on the front page. The superintendent of Olympic National Park in Washington had launched a campaign to remove two aging dams from the Elwha River. The dams were built prior to creation of the park, and one was within its boundaries. The dams had destroyed populations of all five species of salmon, including hundred-pound chinook, that once inhabited the river.

Lujan reportedly hit the roof. The secretary had not been told that an agency of his department was campaigning to take down the dams. Manny's irritation did not make any difference. He was not an influential manager, and agencies of his department had irons in the fire. The National Park Service plowed ahead with environmental studies designed to justify the move. The Fish and Wildlife Service supported removal of the dams, mindful that Indians on the lower Elwha River could mount a lawsuit if something wasn't done to bring back their fish.

The Park Service was active on mountaintops as well as rivers. When Franklin D. Roosevelt pushed through park legislation in 1938, Olympic National Park inherited a population of mountain goats. The goats were not native to the park but had been introduced as a game animal. In the early 1990s, the park superintendent declared that the goats should be shot because they were eating and rolling around on alpine plants unique to high ridges of the eastern Olympic Mountains.

The Park Service has since engaged in a costly, protracted,

and inconclusive struggle with the Fund for the Animals, a national animal-rights group. Even if the agency prevails—and shoots every goat in the park—goats will still inhabit the Olympic Mountains. A portion of the range is in the Olympic National Forest, under jurisdiction of the Department of Agriculture. The Park Service and the Forest Service have different missions. Hence, on the western flanks of 6,911-foot Mount Buckhorn in the park, goats are seen as a menace. On the eastern side of the mountain, national forest land, the shaggy beasts are welcomed as game and not as a threat to plants.

The Forest Service is defined by a slogan familiar from entrance signs to national forests: "Land of Many Uses." The idea, dating from Gifford Pinchot, was that recreation and wildlife and timber harvesting and mining could all coexist. Some agency bureaucrats have carried the philosophy to extremes, believing that all uses can be crammed onto every acre of ground. I've never seen people enjoying a picnic in an open-pit mine. I've never found a clear-cut that benefited a salmon run. Choices have to be made.

The National Park Service has somewhat contradictory missions as well. It is charged with preserving natural wonders under its protection while providing for public enjoyment of same. Increasingly, conflicts arise between these missions, from the battle over expanding the North Rim lodge at the Grand Canyon to eliminating the much-photographed mountain goats on Hurricane Ridge in the Olympics.

The Park Service has also grown doctrinaire. In protecting wild creatures, the philosophy of park managers, as well as much of the environmental community, could be expressed in the final line of a familiar Catholic, Episcopal, and Lutheran prayer: "As it was in the beginning, is now, and ever shall be, world without end."

I'm an old Lutheran, but I can buy into part of that. There are places that should remain forever as they are now. But other parts of the natural environment have been changed irrevocably.

In the as-in-the-beginning category is the coastal plain of the Arctic National Wildlife Refuge on Alaska's North Slope. The windy tundra, at the edge of the Beaufort Sea, is calving ground to the mighty Porcupine Caribou Herd. A bevy of predators, notably wolves, follow the herd and find in it a prime food source.

With the Alaska congressional delegation beating the drums, aided by the best public relations help money can buy, the petroleum industry has fought to open the wildlife refuge to oil and gas drilling. They've told Congress the existing Trans-Alaska Pipeline has not jeopardized its wild neighbors. Ex-oilman George Bush talked about caribou rubbing up against the pipeline and having babies beside it, delivering the unforgettable Bushism: "There's more damned caribou than you can shake a stick at."

I've been up to Prudhoe Bay, heard the industry dog and pony shows, and been suitably impressed by the indoor jogging track at the living quarters for British Petroleum's employees. I have also come away unconvinced. Air and water pollution problems at Prudhoe Bay are more serious than generally believed. Predators have vanished from areas around the pipeline and existing oil development. Platforms and roads and pipelines might well disrupt migration of the Porcupine herd.

Ultimately it comes down to a choice of values. Here lives the greatest herd of wildlife in North America, a sight that takes the breath away and suggests how the continent was in the beginning when man first crossed the Bering land bridge from Asia. Measured against that is a one-in-five chance that exploration platforms will find enough oil to make for a viable venture. If it is economical to extract, the oil patch will yield enough to meet the nation's energy needs for a few months or at most a year.

I TEND TO BE A DEFENDER OF ENDANGERED CRITTERS that have an ongoing claim to the turf, particularly in places where a bird or fish or once-feared predator is squeezed by encroachments and needs a little space to hunt and roam. On private land around Yellowstone National Park, a variety of resorts are expanding or on the drawing boards. A couple of projects have laid out plans for golf courses and vacation homes in the middle of migration corridors used by grizzly bears.

The grizzlies should be allowed to play through. They were around first. They are more legitimately at home than a wealthy tourist, whose existence won't be threatened by having to tee off in the next valley. I'm reminded of what Wilson, Wyoming, rancher Jake Kittle once observed: "The rich don't come here for nature. They come here to be rich." With a few notable exceptions—Ted Turner and Harrison Ford come to mind—that holds true in places like Bozeman, Montana, and Jackson, Wyoming.

Small grizzly bear populations survive in other places, such as the Cabinet Mountains of western Montana and the Selkirks at the Washington–Idaho–British Columbia border. I was appalled when the Reagan administration blessed plans for oil and gas exploration in the Cabinets and other wilderness areas. The grizzlies of the Selkirks are hanging on in shrinking habitat. The biggest threat to their survival is poaching, by people acting sometimes out of spite and on other occasions for profit. When roads are put in, it means too many pickup trucks and too many gun racks.

But there are limits to how much habitat can be protected. We can't expel man from sizeable tracts of the West in order to reintroduce endangered species. I've seen plans from one environmental group, the Alliance for the Wild Rockies, that would dedicate much of the roadless national forest land in the inland Northwest to grizzly bear recovery. No way, I say, will Homo sapiens agree to such a sweeping lockup.

In Idaho, we've heard demands for closure of the Magruder Corridor, a rough four-wheel-drive road that winds through some of the state's wildest mountain terrain. It cuts between the Selway-Bitterroot Wilderness Area and the Frank Church–River of No Return Wilderness Area. The road represents a clear boundary between my outlook and that of elite preservationists. Assuming their vehicles don't get disemboweled, folks not comfortable with wilderness travel get access to spectacular recreation because of that road. Curiously, that offends the preservationist who wants the land to remain exactly the way God created it, with man not allowed to tread upon it.

I'm not that kind of preservationist. As a conservationist, I want the land protected, restored when necessary—along with its wild creatures—and never destroyed. Still, I want it accessible for fishing, hunting, family camping, and the nonstrenuous walks that can begin a youngster's attachment to nature. I enjoy getting on a horse for a multiday trip into the backcountry; backpacking enthusiasts dominated my staff. But not everybody has an appetite for this, or the time.

As governor, I found myself trying to preserve places, but also trying to protect citizens from the keep-everybody-out-but-us faction. I fought to keep open a handful of airstrips in wilderness areas, both out of safety—central Idaho has vast stretches of mountain and canyon with no airports—and so flyers could land and go fishing and hunting. I had to trust that the 1.2 million people of the aptly named Gem State were not of a mind to mess up its backcountry.

I wonder whether the grizzly bear would be any better off if we acceded to demands of the Alliance for the Wild Rockies: curtailing logging, closing roads, and restricting rural lifestyles. It might make *Ursus horribilis* a hated creature at the very time wildlife managers are finally persuading ranchers to accept the bears' right to exist. Every sonofagun with a rifle would be aiming for them if the bears are seen as villains in a "land grab."

I HAD OCCASIONS TO PICK A FEW FIGHTS AND confrontations, and frankly relished this part of the job. But I also recognized that it is the conscientious officeholder's duty to work out society's compromises. In doing that, you have to recognize—often over bellowed objections from special interest groups—legitimate competing values. Environmental issues are not exempt. When discussing endangered wild creatures, no places prove the point more than the south fork and Henry's fork valleys of the upper Snake River.

The Idaho constitution declares flat out: "The right to divert and appropriate the unappropriated waters of any natural stream to beneficial uses, shall never be denied. . . ." It is a passage that is almost as fundamental to the convictions of eastern Idaho irrigators as the Book of Mormon. In fact, a U.S. Bureau of Reclamation brochure, "How Water Won the West," shows a farm couple standing near Caldwell, Idaho, looking at a sign that reads, "Desert Ranch: Have Faith in God and U.S. Reclamation."

The upper Snake River country is high desert: Most of it gets less than twelve inches of rain a year. "Our climate is Great Basin, not coastal," Perry Swisher, an opponent in the 1966 governor's race and later a damned fine public utility commissioner, likes to tell visitors from the wet side of the mountains.

Out of what farmer Reed Oldham once called "a forbidding land" has come a productive land of irrigated fields, well-kept towns, and conservative voters whose hearts this Democrat finally managed to win over. (In my last reelection race, I carried one heavily Mormon county that had given Ronald Reagan 86 percent of its vote.) The impoundment and diversion of the Snake River made it possible.

There is another vision of the river, shared by increasing numbers of the West's people. It is best summed up in a famous quote from U.S. Supreme Court Justice Oliver Wendell Holmes: "A river is more than an amenity. It is a treasure."

If you want to know what he meant, go to the sixty-nine-mile stretch of the south fork of the Snake River in eastern Idaho, between Palisades Dam and the junction with the Henry's fork. Float on the river, which you can do for miles. Stand beneath the gently swaying cottonwoods and poplars. Or scramble the bluffs above the river, take note of its braided channels, and scan the canyon rim for eagles.

The south fork is home to about fifty bald eagles in summer and twice that number in winter. The resident eagles have built nearly thirty nests along the river, and produce about half of the young hatched each year in the Greater Yellowstone area. So-called transient eagles—an unflattering name to call America's national symbol—range far to the north and west. They come to the south fork from as far distant as Great Slave Lake in the Northwest Territories of Canada. An eagle researcher, Mike Whitfield, banded one bird in the upper Snake River that ended up nearly a thousand miles away at the mouth of the Columbia River.

The south fork is a captivating place. Whitfield uses a scene witnessed one winter to liken the river to *Wild Kingdom*. A pair of bald eagles were copulating atop a tree. Down below, a cougar was spotted hunting near the river. A mountain goat slept on a nearby ledge. Deer, moose, and elk browsed along the banks. Ducks were diving in the water and popping back up again. Canada geese and sandhill cranes were spotted during the day. "This reach of the Snake is to the Rockies what the Everglades are to the Southeast," Tim Palmer wrote in his excellent book *The Snake River: Window to the West*.

It's no secret that I see the south fork as a treasure: It is one of the great cutthroat trout and brown trout fishing streams in the world. The state Fish and Game Department has estimated that thirty-five hundred adult fish live in each mile of river. The trout spawn in side channels and pools. They are a vital component of the food chain that sustains the bald eagles.

Politicians have their biases. I am a fly fisherman; it's a sport at which I've developed skill, and recreation in clear water has provided me with the peace and serenity needed for clear thought. Of course, I've reflected the angler's point of view in decisions about rivers and resources. It has provided a counterbalance to agencies with other agendas.

In my state, there have been multiple conflicts between the values of irrigation and those of a natural river, and nowhere more than on the upper reaches of the Snake River. The Bureau of Reclamation controls the flow of the river through release of water impounded behind its upstream dams. The bureau is an Interior Department agency, but with a culture worlds apart from the National Park Service.

Environmental laws or no environmental laws, the Bureau of Reclamation sees irrigators as its constituency and their satisfaction as its responsibility and legal duty. The agency recognizes other water needs—accepts their legitimacy—but always within the context of impounding enough water to deal with a drought. When it considers a river like the Snake that depends on yearly runoff, BuRec is forever driven by a fear that there will not be enough water.

I've spent years negotiating with and trying to cajole BuRec officials. When pushed, they usually covered their fannies with a pair of explanations.

First, they could, if they wanted—by the legalities of state water laws—dry up the Snake River. It was only thanks to the good offices of BuRec and irrigators that *any* flow levels were provided in the river. "If you need our help, politely ask and we will see what we can do. If you dare make demands, we will do nothing."

And, second, the water in their reservoirs belonged to the irrigators and must be paid for before it could be released to increase river flows. If reservoirs were lowered in midwinter to save wildlife, there was no assurance of enough snow to fill them up again. "We would be liable."

The fear of losing water rights, and a mania to maintain control, is central to BuRec's way of thinking. The dry, cold winter of 1987–88 revealed the narrowness of that mind-set, when BuRec washed its hands of responsibilities to the south fork of the Snake River.

In the late fall of '88, the river flow entering Palisades Reservoir was about 2,200 cubic feet per second. As it refilled the reservoir, BuRec released only 750 cubic feet per second down the river. It kept to that flow regime from November until the end of March. During summer and fall, the river had been filled from bank to bank, with water in side channels where cutthroat trout spawn. Now, the river below the dam was reduced to a small main channel. The side channels were dry, except for small pools, with no water running in and out. And this is where the young fish live.

An estimated six hundred thousand cutthroat and brown trout died—a majority less than two years of age—along with the insect larvae that is their food source. The ripple effect was felt along the food chain. In trees above the river, the number of eaglets dropped from two to one per nest.

A similar debacle unfolded a year later on the nearby Henry's fork, home to hundreds of rare trumpeter swans that spend winters below Island Park Dam. They spend the cold months on the river in expectation that upstream hot springs will assure an unfrozen channel. The swans feed on tubers and aquatic plants. The river nearly froze up during the same winter that thousands of trout were dying on the south fork. The Bureau of Reclamation was warned that as many as one-third of the five hundred wintering trumpeter swans would die were the river to freeze over. BuRec didn't budge: It had a reservoir to fill. A senior official, pulling himself up to full bureaucratic officiousness, declared, "There are claims on that water."

Henry's fork froze up the following winter. As many as one hundred trumpeter swans died, a boon only to another species lately deprived of its food source. "We ended up with eagles feeding on dead trumpeter swans, one endangered species eating a more endangered species," Whitfield recalled.

There was a public outcry: With people asking unwelcome questions about who ran the river, BuRec was finally moved to action. Irrigators made a "donation" of water. The Idaho Nature Conservancy bought water from farmers—enough to flush the river and restore some flow. The remainder of the swans survived.

The death of the swans could have been averted if only a bit more water had been released into Henry's fork, an action that would have required just a little vision and daring from the Bureau of Reclamation. It turned out that the reservoir was easily refilled by late winter snows. The Nature Conservancy got its money back.

The response to species depends on the agency. Faced with the nation's most absolute environmental law, the National Park Service has chosen to go aggressively after mountain goats. The Bureau of Reclamation obstinately resisted adequate river flows for swans and trout. I'm wary of both attitudes, and impatient with the fears of irrigators that they will lose control and with the excessive demands from groups like the Alliance for the Wild Rockies.

I HOPE FOR CONSTRUCTIVE AMENDMENT OF THE Endangered Species Act, especially incentives for private landowners to assume some of the burden of protecting critters on their property. Obligations of protection fall inordinately on federal lands. And that means the West. About 64 percent of Idaho is owned by the federal government, and the percentage is even higher in Alaska and Utah.

Unfortunately, most of the "reform" proposals I've seen give landowners loopholes instead of incentives, and would turn preservation decisions into political tugs-of-war. In one bill, the secretary of the interior would get to play God: He or she would decide whether a species should be restored, left to fend for itself, or allowed to go extinct. At present, of course, the secretary has to develop a recovery plan for all species deemed to be endangered.

When I was interior secretary, I never hankered after God's job. His life and death powers are too sweeping. In heaven, presumably, there are no hardball pressure tactics. Washington, D.C., is someplace else again. Science surely does yield to politics. In future Republican administrations, we'd probably have species condemned to extinction in order to appease ultraconservative Western politicians. With the Democrats, we might see totally impractical restoration schemes adopted as a sop to militant preservationists.

If you have any doubt of that, look at the Forest Service, one federal agency so buffeted by politicians and pressure groups that it cannot chart its own course or fully benefit from the skills of its own people on the ground. The Forest Service oversees more than 160 million acres of land, most of it in the West. Nearly 40 percent of Idaho is in national forests, including Hells Canyon, the Sawtooth and White Cloud Mountains, and our great wild Salmon River.

Mobilized to meet the nation's post–World War II housing boom, the Forest Service donned loggers boots. Each national forest was supposedly a "Land of Many Uses," but one use predominated throughout the West—timber production.

It was, for instance, the Forest Service that campaigned to expand logging in Alaska's Tongass National Forest. It signed long-term sweetheart timber sales deals that established big, polluting pulp mills in Ketchikan and Sitka. The great forests and wildlife habitats of Admiralty Island were to have sustained a third mill in Juneau. A lawsuit stopped it—thank God!—and most of the island was protected as a national monument in the Alaska Lands Act.

By midcentury the logging culture was ingrained in the West; witness the landmark environmental battles of the 1960s and early 1970s in Washington state. The Forest Service used every device at its disposal, unsuccessfully as it turned out, to prevent the creation of North Cascades National Park. It tried to promote an octopus-shaped plan for a Glacier Peak Wilderness Area, leaving out forests but "protecting" the volcano's glaciers and surrounding ridges. When leaders of outdoors clubs went to see the supervisor of the Wenatchee National Forest to talk about the Alpine Lakes region—a land of six hundred mountain lakes in the Cascades, easily accessible from Seattle—they were given the famous greeting, "Just what do you people want?" As Congress took up wilderness legislation, the Forest Service legislated by bulldozer. Logging roads were driven into places sought for preservation.

Starting in the 1960s, Congress tried to steer the Forest Service in a different direction, a task that proved as difficult as turning an ocean liner around. The Multiple-Use Sustained-Yield Act of 1960 declared that national forests would be administered "for outdoor recreation, timber, watershed, and wildlife and fish purposes." It didn't stop the Forest Service from clear-cutting steep slopes on the south fork of the Salmon River, triggering what researchers gently called "mass soil movement" that wiped out a prized salmon run.

Congress was not through. It passed the landmark Wilderness Act in 1964, and set down further requirements of environmental protection when it enacted the National Forest Management Act of 1976. The Forest Service was directed to manage its lands so as to "provide for diversity of plant and animal communities based on the suitability and capability of the specific land area. . . ."

The culture of the Forest Service began to change in the late 1970s. It wasn't apparent in Washington, D.C., where timber bureaucrats reigned and resisted reform. They helped thwart my efforts to transfer the agency out of the Agriculture Department and into Interior Department jurisdiction. But I had seen a change in the field. As governor, I initiated an annual horseback trip with my state's national forest supervisors. They turned out to be quite a mix. Collectively, everybody usually gave the party line. The group included a number of proud loggers who were hostile to anyone perceived as a tree-hugger. However, as I rode with these guys, I was also able to pick out professionals who were committed to making the new rules work, intent on not letting logging crowd out other uses, and enthusiastic about new forest users.

The evolution of forest policy was brought to a screeching halt by the Reagan administration. The advent of the Gipper and George Bush, the "environmental president" who followed him, produced a kind of chain-reaction collision in national forest management.

An order to increase timber sales ran head-on into requirements of the National Forest Management Act and the Endangered Species Act. The pressure exerted by politicians in Washington, D.C., to cut more trees butted into the drive for balance advocated by a new generation of forest managers.

During the Reagan years, the visage of James Watt, my successor as interior secretary, launched hundreds of political cartoons and decorated dozens of membership recruitment mailings by environmental groups. Very little attention was paid, however, to Assistant Agriculture Secretary John Crowell, the former Louisiana-Pacific executive who became overseer of the Forest Service's vast domain. He was stepping up the timber cut and putting in place policies that seemed designed to transform national forests into industry tree farms.

In coastal forests from northern California to Washington, the national forest timber cut was pushed up to record levels. All old-growth trees outside of wilderness areas were marked for liquidation. The ancient trees came down at a rate of more than sixty thousand acres a year.

In the inland Northwest, meanwhile, politicians were allowed to run wild. Forest Service managers found themselves under pressure to jack up logging levels so high that they could not protect grizzly habitat, elk calving grounds, or bull trout spawning areas. Caught in the middle, they could not meet their legal obligations to protect endangered species or ensure diversity.

The consequences were not long in coming. On March 7, 1991, U.S. District Judge William L. Dwyer, in Seattle, declared unlawful the Forest Service's plans to log habitat of the endangered northern spotted owl. The judge delivered a blistering attack on the agency and on logging of coastal national forests: "After decades of logging and development, perhaps ten percent of the original old growth forest remains. . . . The owl is an indicator species. . . . Its waxing or waning is a viability measure for other wildlife—for an ecosystem—in the remaining old growth."

With Dwyer's ruling, the logging of federal lands west of the Cascade Range came to a virtual halt. The Bush administration could not come up with a viable plan to protect the small nocturnal bird or its old-growth habitat. Less than six months later, John Mumma, the Forest Service's regional forester for the northern Rockies—including the Nez Perce National Forest—quit his job in protest against pressure from above. In testimony before a House committee, he was every bit as blunt as Dwyer: "My supervisors and district rangers in the Northern region recognize that we cannot meet my timber targets. I also believe that my superiors in the Forest Service recognize that I cannot meet my targets or sell more timber. . . . I have done everything I can to meet all of my targets. I have failed to reach the quotas only because to do so would have required me to violate federal law. . . ."

The pressure wasn't subtle. Idaho, Montana, and Wyoming senators have drawn a bead on forest supervisors. While obeying the law, Tom Kovalicky, the Nez Perce supervisor, was selling between 75 million and 100 million board feet of timber a year, the sales going through without time-consuming administrative and legal appeals from environmental groups. The reward for his work? Senators James McClure and Steve Symms tried to get him fired, or kicked upstairs and out of line management. Tom flew back to Washington, D.C., and faced down Symms.

"I understand you are asking the chief [of the Forest Service] to fire me," he told Idaho's junior senator.

"Why, Tom, there's no one here trying to fire you," replied Symms. Somebody should have measured the length of his nose at that point.

The Clinton administration, to its credit, has tried to clean up the mess. In the spring of 1993, the president hosted a day-long timber summit in Portland, and came up with a plan for a much lower level of logging and the conservation of the spotted owl's old-growth habitat. Dubbed Option 9, it passed muster with Judge Dwyer, but not before the plan was hit by lawsuits from *both* the Northwest Forest Resource Council, representing loggers and mill owners, and the Seattle Audubon Society.

With flak coming from all sides, however, the administration was slow to get timber sales into the pipeline and to put dollars into remote rural communities needing to retool their economies. Timber towns felt bypassed and resentful, even in a region that in other fields was enjoying an unprecedented boom in jobs.

As interior secretary, Bruce Babbitt has undertaken a steady, productive courtship of state agencies and private landowners—from timber companies to real estate developers. He has succeeded in negotiating a series of long-term habitat conservation plans. Although worked out in hairsplitting detail by legions of lawyers, these plans are rooted in a simple John Lennon lyric: "All we are saying is give peace a chance."

Such once-rapacious outfits as the Plum Creek Timber Company understand that old logging practices aren't compatible with the West's new land ethic. They are correcting old ways and still staying viable. They recognize, sometimes reluctantly, the wide public support for environmental laws, and have adapted environment-friendly forest practices.

The plans do basic, sensible things: safeguarding places where salmon fry and baby elk are born, assuring wildlife of year-round places to eat, recognizing the routes animals and fish use to migrate, and protecting streamside and in-stream habitat.

Old animosities die hard, however. Drawing up maps on the use of lands is about as easy in the American West as it is in Bosnia. Babbitt recently visited Seattle to sign a fifty-year habitat conservation accord on timberlands owned by the state of Washington. The ink wasn't dry before the Northwest Ecosystem Alliance claimed the plan gave too much latitude to loggers. Meanwhile, the Northwest Forestry Association argued that protection measures would make it impossible to meet timber sales targets.

My old friend Kovalicky, retired from the Forest Service, summed it up colorfully over coffee in Grangeville: "It seems like they want to give us an either-or choice: We can cut the shit out of a place, salmon can't have babies, and we send the soil all the way to the Pacific Ocean—or we lock it up and don't let anybody in."

Chapter 7

THE LIFE
OF A DECISION

ITTING IN THE GOVERNOR'S CHAIR FOR
fourteen years, I insisted on satisfying a simple, basic pair of
questions before putting my name on any measure sent to
me by the Idaho Legislature: Whose lives will be affected by this
bill, and how?

Never did I grapple with more complex implications of such
straightforward questions than in the early spring of 1990, when
sitting on my desk was the most sweeping, restrictive anti-abortion legislation yet to be passed by lawmakers in any state.

I found myself, a happily married family man with three
grown daughters and two granddaughters, trying to understand
the anguish of a teenage girl who is the victim of a date rape, or
incest at the hands of a father or stepfather. What would be her
burdens? What tugs at her conscience as she decides whether to
report the crime? Or end the pregnancy? Would requirements in
this legislation compound the horrors of a situation that to me
was almost unthinkable? Were such burdens on an individual
enough to outweigh what I saw as society's fundamental duty to
protect life?

The thinking had to be done in a circuslike atmosphere of
jammed phone lines, crude pressure tactics, and jingoism that
did no justice to complex moral and ethical issues that demanded
conscience as well as political calculation.

Idaho had been chosen as a legal and political laboratory by a
bevy of national anti-abortion groups. Several other states, even
conservative Utah, had rebuffed them. They needed to find a legislature that would enact carefully crafted legal language
designed, in essence, to nullify *Roe v. Wade*, the 1973 Supreme
Court ruling that had legalized abortion across the country.

The state law could be used as a nationwide test vehicle in
which, they hoped, a more conservative U.S. Supreme Court
would lay to rest its earlier ruling. Other states would then be
free to follow the pattern of Idaho's law. With William Rehnquist

presiding as chief justice, Antonin Scalia and Anthony Kennedy recently named to the court, and Sandra Day O'Connor hinting at a willingness to affirm state restrictions on abortion, the plan to approach the high court was designed with a high likelihood of success.

Idaho seemed to fit the bill as a state where the right-to-life movement could write a law, get it passed, and tailor the antici-pated Supreme Court test. In 1990, we had a conservative, Republican-dominated legislature. The state's largest religious groupings, taking in well over one-third of the population, were Mormons and Roman Catholics. Mormon legislators tended to vote as a bloc on abortion issues. I am a Democrat and a Lutheran, but had not varied from a pro-life position throughout a twenty-nine-year political career. If I dared hesitate, many felt I would be called to account in my rapidly approaching reelection campaign.

Drafted out of state, on a model drawn up by the National Right to Life Committee, the anti-abortion legislation worked its way through the legislature early in 1990. The sponsors assumed I would sign it. Curiously, they never came to talk with me about their bill or its national objectives.

The measure would have banned all abortions except in cases of rape reported to police within seven days, incest (but only if the victim was under eighteen), severe fetal deformity, or threat to the physical health of the mother. As the bill was written, a woman who had been raped could be refused an abortion if her claim was challenged by the alleged rapist. On the eighth day, if a woman had failed to report a rape, she could face criminal penal-ties if she sought to terminate the pregnancy.

The legislation would have outlawed an estimated 95 percent of the 1,700 pregnancy terminations performed annually in Idaho. Physicians who violated major provisions of the measure would have faced civil fines of up to $10,000—rising to $50,000 by the third offense—and civil lawsuits by the father or anyone else given standing in the case, like the parent of a minor child or a county prosecutor. If a woman sought an abortion, she would have faced a $10,000 fine.

IT'S TOUGH FOR ME TO ADMIT EVEN YEARS LATER, but the bill was halfway through the legislature before I sat down and read it. Abortion was an issue I felt to be unambiguous, and I thought my position was clear. I was opposed to abortion in all cases except rape, incest, or a threat to the life of the mother.

My lesson in the complexities of this legislation began at a staff meeting in early March, just after the state house of representatives approved the abortion bill.

"Well, I've been of the assumption that I'll probably sign it," I told my staff. "I'm pro-life, after all."

"Have you studied it?" asked Marc Johnson, then my press secretary and later my chief of staff.

I saw the merit of his question when I sat down with the bill later that day. I realized that the state would face a monumental decision. Outsiders were seeking to write out a course of action for us. The intent of the proposed law—to restrict abortion— probably had the support of most Idaho citizens, but were its provisions wise and just? I would have to make the call, but I wanted the people of the state to pause, reflect, and understand what was at stake.

Politicians toss around a lot of prose about how to make tough decisions. Perhaps my favorite comes from Canada's former Prime Minister Pierre Trudeau, who once said: "What does one do? One does one's duty, of course."

Of course, hell! Coming to a clear idea of one's duty, particularly in the vortex of controversy, can be devilishly difficult. I had always operated under the guidelines of educating myself, trying to listen to all sides, sleeping on a decision, and being able to face myself in the morning once that decision was made. My inclination was to act quickly. I had confidence my decision would stand. Although always controlled by the other party, the legislature mustered the votes to override only one of my 138 vetoes during four terms in office.

In the case of abortion, that orderly process was not possible. The pressure tactics and cacophony of noise made quiet listening exceedingly difficult. I had to listen to sometimes bizarre arguments. One fellow called me up and declared, with almost Biblical certitude, "I'm a medical doctor and I find it impossible to believe that any woman can conceive by rape."

As if such reasoning weren't enough, the abortion debate even enveloped Idaho's number one crop. Molly Yard, president of the National Organization for Women, announced that supporters of reproductive rights would boycott Idaho potatoes if the anti-abortion bill became law. They drove home the point by dumping ten thousand pounds of potatoes on the steps of the capitol.

In response, pro-life forces across the land vowed to triple their consumption of spuds if I would just sign the bill or let it become law. Beverly LaHaye, president of Concerned Women of America, declared: "We are calling for the massive increase of purchases of Idaho potatoes."

Jim Hawkins, our state Commerce Department director, fretted to me that the abortion issue could imperil Idaho's economic revival. It was, as Hawkins told the *New York Times*, "the damnedest thing I've ever seen in my life. One minute somebody calls up with a big business order saying they'll cancel it if the governor signs the bill. The next minute, it's just the opposite."

Clumsy boycott threats would have been amusing were it not for the fact that people could draw a bead on the Idaho economy. Tourism earns the Gem State $1.5 billion a year. Idaho producers

annually sell 135 million pounds of potatoes. Spuds constitute a
$650 million chunk of our economy. I doubt very much that
McDonald's customers would have been demanding to know
where their fries came from, but such threats resonate in the hot-
house atmosphere of a nationally watched debate.

As it turned out, I had plenty of time to think about consequences of the abortion bill, in part because I couldn't get any
other work done. Once I indicated that my mind was not made
up, there was no place where I could escape from the issue. As I
cleaned up the yard at home one Sunday afternoon, a motorist
braked her car, rolled down the window, and gave me a piece of
her mind.

A national barrage of phone calls targeted me almost from
the minute that our state senate passed the measure and sent it to
the governor's office. My office number was given out on the radio
by Focus on the Family and other conservative organizations. The
governor's office in Boise was usually an easy, informal place.
During the last days of March, however, we were receiving more
than two thousand phone calls a day. It was impossible to get a
call into or out of the office. My office was even the recipient of a
hoax phone message, allegedly from Mother Teresa, sternly
admonishing me to sign the bill. It turned out she was in the
mountains of India, and incommunicado. That didn't stop Washington, D.C., columnist Bob Novak from writing that I had
refused to accept a phone call from Mother Teresa.

As I began to sort through the decision, however, one political
fact immediately stood out: The passion of advocates, on both sides
of the abortion issue, obscured the ambivalent attitudes that a
majority of Americans hold toward the termination of pregnancies.

Perhaps one-fourth of the population holds to the view that
the life of an unborn child should be protected at all costs,
including harm to the physical and mental health of the mother.
Another 25 percent likely accept the argument of a woman's

right to choose, and support abortion on demand.

A much larger percentage—probably a majority in both Idaho and the country as a whole—find themselves uncomfortable with the extremes and somewhat resentful that such a personal question has become the subject of political debate and governmental intrusion. If pressed, a majority will come down in favor of personal choice. But that does not translate to endorsing abortion on demand, especially after fetal viability.

Those taking a middle view comprise a very silent majority in the abortion debate. They are, however, perceptive and wise in their judgments. They understand the gravity of the issue. They respect personal conviction. They refuse zealots' calls to punish an officeholder who believes in a position and holds to it, even if they disagree with his or her stand. But they are merciless on politicians who change position out of expediency. I watched in 1989 as a pair of Republican gubernatorial candidates, J. Marshall Coleman in Virginia and Jim Courter in New Jersey, were waxed by the voters after wavering in their pro-life views.

My duty as a governor, one who was to face the voters seven months hence, was to make clear my position of conscience on abortion, and that my conscience would not be reshaped in response to any poll or pressure tactic. I also played out the deliberative process. Of course, I wanted the time to think through my decision. By watching the lengthy reflection of a usually decisive politician, the people would come to appreciate that that this was a weighty matter.

While my views on abortion were dictated by conscience, my decision on the anti-abortion bill would be heavily influenced by the measure's consequences. It was a case of obligations in conflict.

IN MY VIEW, LIFE BEGINS AT CONCEPTION. THE FETUS may not be viable for months to come, but the potential in that unborn child is present from that moment. A new life has been created. The protection of life is the fundamental reason that people first banded together to form societies. It anchors what philosophers call the "social contract"; people come together collectively to do what they cannot do well as individuals. The first and foremost reason we have a society and its various governments is to help protect a person's life, assuring that he or she can enjoy the liberty and pursue the happiness guaranteed in the U.S. Constitution.

For this reason, I have long felt that we all have a stake in protecting life, particularly the young and the unborn. I was never comfortable with the Supreme Court's decision, in 1973, that personal freedom took precedence over society's interest in life. But there are circumstances, although rare, in which society and government should grant an individual the right to assert the personal interest, and in which the individual's stake is transcendent over the greater public good.

In the case of abortion, these circumstances are where the pregnancy is the result of rape or incest, and where the mother's physical life or mental health is truly endangered by carrying the child through to birth. There are two bodies involved in a pregnancy, two lives that will be impacted. Society has an interest in both.

The bill before me clearly asserted that the life of the unborn child carried precedence over the life of the mother. An element of equity and fairness—and, above all, compassion—was lacking.

I reflected on the practical effects of the measure. A victim of rape or incest often agonizes for weeks before even approaching a loved one with the dreadful news. Giving someone a week to report the crime to the police was cruel and obtuse. The possibility of a battle over the future of a fetus, pitting the victim against her alleged rapist, would certainly lead to fewer rapes being reported to police.

In my heart, then, I found that I could not compound what was for some women a personal tragedy by making them, or their physicians, face criminal sanctions. The tragedy would also strike disproportionately at the poor. Those who could afford it would simply cross the state line into Washington or Oregon and obtain a legal abortion.

I resolved to veto the bill. When doing so, however, I committed myself to delivering a message that would not fit into anybody's jingoism. I was not endorsing abortion. The bill would have prevented the termination of pregnancies in desperate conditions. In less drastic circumstances, where the pregnancy was unintended or unwanted, I believe people are responsible for facing up to the consequences of a decision to have sex without taking the appropriate precautions.

No young couple is done a favor when, if we permit abortion on demand, we say in effect that they do not have to take responsibility for their actions. One of the greatest struggles we face as a society is just this notion of accountability for our actions—of accountability to our families, our society, our God, and ourselves.

Permitting abortion on demand goes in the face of accountability, saying that a person does not have to take into account the other life and that the person's own interests are more important than the unborn or society's. To me, advocates of freedom to choose are declaring a right to be totally egocentric, to be totally selfish, to be totally irresponsible. I don't accept that.

Society has, however, an obligation to mother and child. If the baby is conceived out of the parent's irresponsibility, the child should not be punished. A sharp-tongued abortion rights supporter, Representative Barney Frank of Massachusetts, spoke an uncomfortable truth a few years back when he declared that for some pro-life advocates, life seems to begin at conception and end at birth. It is unconscionable to me that Senator Jesse Helms could crusade to restrict abortions while seeking to cut back money for child nutrition programs. We must have measures to aid women and children with pre- and postnatal care, with early childhood nutrition programs, with early childhood health screening. We should provide more support for child care and make it possible for teenage mothers to complete high school.

Sex education should be a part of that schooling. I don't like it, but lots of parents have been dumping the job on the public schools. So, with parental approval, I believe we should start sex education courses in primary schools. The subject should be taught in the context of an expression of values and choices, and with the inescapable lesson that actions have consequences. We have responsibility for those consequences. I do not believe the argument of some that contraception leads to promiscuity. We should educate kids in values, but also recognize the power of hormones. Contraceptives should be available to sexually active teens, even through counselors' offices at schools.

As I worked through the complexity of the abortion measure, both personal and societal, my blood began to boil at how Idaho had become a guinea pig for this legislation.

The state was fully capable of making its own judgments about abortion, and could have drafted a far more humane set of restrictions than those dictated by sponsors beyond our boundaries. The provisions were not written with sensitivity to the plight of a teenage rape victim. Instead, the drafting was done with an eye to meeting conditions on how states could restrict abortions, conditions hinted at by Supreme Court Justice O'Connor in the *Webster v. Planned Parenthood* ruling. The compounding of pain to a rape or incest victim in Idaho was subordinated to the courtship of a Supreme Court justice in Washington, D.C.

The National Right to Life Committee was nothing but up-front about its objective. The group threatened to withdraw support for the Idaho bill if it was rewritten in any way. As our state senate wound up debate, the group's Western director, Brian Johnson, declared to a reporter: "What we're after here is Sandra Day O'Connor. We know Justice O'Connor wants to overturn *Roe v. Wade*. We just have to give her something she's comfortable with."

He was wrong, both about O'Connor—who voted to uphold the essence of the 1973 ruling in a later case—and about me. During the decision-making process, I had consulted with Brigham Young University law professor Richard Wilkins. Wilkins, a critic of *Roe*, told me that the Idaho bill was far too restrictive to pass muster with the Supreme Court.

AT AN EVENING NEWS CONFERENCE IN BOISE, AMIDST cries of "Shame!" from bill supporters, I announced and explained the veto. "Somebody thought Idaho looks like a patsy," I declared. "I submit to you: Idaho is not a patsy."

I went over the reasoning, saying the bill was so narrowly drawn that it would punitively and without compassion further harm an Idaho woman who might find herself in the horrible, unthinkable position of confronting a pregnancy that resulted from rape or incest.

The legislature had recessed for the year, so there was no effort at a veto override. It would, of course, have failed. I knew how to count noses even while I was examining my conscience.

Advocates of the bill vowed to take their revenge and pre-dicted my defeat in November. *The Hotline*, a national political newsletter, day after day speculated over the political cost of my action, and whether TV adman Robert Squier was capable of res-cuing my campaign.

A strange thing happened, however, predictable only with 20-20 hindsight: The veto of that anti-abortion bill cemented my reelection in November.

The Andrus family is not of one mind on abortion. My

daughter Tracy has always been pro-choice. She felt, however, that in the interests of political survival I should have signed the bill, allowing the federal courts to shoot it down.

The veto brought tears of joy to Tracy's eyes and was, in her words, "one of the proudest moments of my life." But there were tears of sadness in the eyes of another longtime friend, an abortion opponent who had urged me to sign the legislation.

For those on both sides, however, the deliberation with which I approached the issue and made the decision somehow conveyed to the electorate that I was a guy who could be trusted.

My Republican opponent, Roger Fairchild, declared that he would have signed the legislation "in a baby's heartbeat" and tried to cash in on the issue by sending a fund-raising letter to the mailing list of Right to Life of Idaho. The letter accused me of abandoning my pro-life convictions.

The voters didn't believe him for a New York minute. I was able to explain, with wide public acceptance, "I sign good bills. I don't sign bad bills."

I won a landslide victory with 70 percent of the vote, carrying all but two counties and winning even heavily Mormon towns in eastern Idaho that used to give Ronald Reagan 85 percent of the vote. A heavy turnout of pro-choice voters bounced several of the state legislators who had sponsored the anti-abortion bill.

It seemed like a satisfying end but for subsequent, unsettling developments.

Governor Buddy Roemer of Louisiana had a similar bill come to his desk a year later, and vetoed it. He became an immediate target for punishment by some in the Republican Party. Roemer was defeated for reelection, running third in the primary behind ethically challenged Democrat Edwin Edwards and former Ku Klux Klan leader David Duke.

Nationally, the Republican Party moved toward exactly the

kind of dogmatic, inhumane abortion position that was embodied in the Idaho bill. I recoiled at Pat Buchanan's "cultural war" speech at the GOP's Houston convention.

Something curiously similar happened in the Democratic Party, despite a warning signed by nearly fifty Democrats in Congress that the party should not close its doors to those who believe life begins at conception. The party identified itself so stridently with the abortion-on-demand position that Pennsylvania Governor Robert Casey, an abortion opponent, was denied the right to speak at its 1992 convention.

In Idaho two years earlier, voters had trusted me while perhaps disagreeing with my veto. I see fewer and fewer examples of an electorate giving such slack.

Voters used to respect the judgment of their leaders, particularly in the West. Montana was a fervent New Deal state, but stood behind Senator Burton Wheeler when he opposed Franklin D. Roosevelt's court-packing plan. Idaho was hawkish on the Vietnam War, but reelected Senator Frank Church in 1968 and 1974.

Sad to say, however, politicians of stature have fallen victim to wedge issues in which a political consultant isolates a vote, or an unpopular stand, and ruthlessly twists it. Particularly on abortion, people who might otherwise have a good shot at the White House are denied the opportunity to compete because they do not toe the party line.

Leaders of the religious right vowed an all-out campaign to block retired General Colin Powell had he run for the Republican presidential nomination in 1996. Senator Alan Simpson of Wyoming would have made an ideal Republican running mate for George Bush in 1988, but was bumped from consideration because of his pro-choice views. Representative Lindy Boggs of Louisiana was an early entrant in the Democrats' 1984 veep sweepstakes, but her pro-life position caused her name to sink quickly.

Curiously, although my religious roots are in the Reformation, several of my top aides over the years were devout Catholics. They were, to a person, committed to the causes of social justice and economic opportunity that distinguish the Democratic Party. They also accepted the teachings of their church on the protection of life. Will this position of conscience and religious conviction make it impossible for them ever to run for office as Democrats?

I hope not, but fear I may be wrong. It hurts in today's political climate to be sensitive, reflective, and moderate. The seed money in political campaigns is often supplied by issue advocacy groups. They demand adherence to a set-in-stone position. As Senator Eugene McCarthy of Minnesota once quipped, these people aren't satisfied with breast beating but demand nothing less than indecent exposure.

It runs to both sides of the political spectrum. The quick-sound-bite culture of politics works against someone with a measured, deliberate position like my 1990 stand on the abortion bill. The consultant–hit man can always simplify a position in order to tear it down.

In this era of political polarization, however, Idaho's 1990 abortion debate does carry a lesson. The vast majority of people can be persuaded to respect consistent, coherent, long-held, and well-articulated beliefs. It takes a helluva lot of skillful persuading, however.

Chapter 8

FEEDING
THE SHARKS

S A PREEMINENT TWENTIETH-CENTURY
revolutionary, Mao Zedong once declared that political
power flows out of the barrel of a gun. It would
be hard to find anybody, except maybe the Montana Militia,
who still believes that maxim. In the post-Mao world, power is
transmitted through the lens of a television camera and the
Internet.

My thirty-four-year career in public life coincided with a
rapid succession of jolts that forever transformed the means of
communication. The transformation was particularly jarring for
those of us in government. Dealing with the press and shaping
public opinion is a vital part of being a politician.

I first ran for the state legislature in 1960, when candidates
were still made or broken by the printed word. It was an era
that ended on the September night when John F. Kennedy and
Richard Nixon squared off in their first debate. The youthful
Massachusetts senator won over the audience while the vice
president seemed to concentrate on winning debating points.
Television replaced newspapers, and TV studio events sup-
planted rallies, as the nation's principal instruments of campaigning and, later, governing. "Speech is obsolete as a means of
communication," Nixon would tell aides when he again sought
the White House.

Over the decades that followed, the tube's attention span
grew steadily shorter, and unfortunately television seemed to take
the nation with it. When I plotted my first run for governor in
the mid-1960s, David Brinkley would use wry humor to start off
a story on Lyndon Johnson or Barry Goldwater airing on the
nation's dominant evening news program. And then Brinkley
would add: "Here is a little bit of what he said." The president or
candidate would be allowed to talk for thirty or forty seconds. In
the three decades since, however, the average "sound bite" has
shrunk to less than seven seconds. President Clinton is lucky to

get five seconds on the network morning shows. What can you say in seven seconds? Very little. Can you convey a serious message? Not much chance. In many a politician's campaign, public communication has become an exercise in aides thinking up snappy phrases, and the candidate memorizing lines.

TV reporting of politics, particularly by the networks, has come to concentrate on whatever trivial scandal momentarily absorbs Washington, D.C. The result is a striking disconnection between political coverage and the issues and decisions that affect the lives of ordinary people.

Walter Cronkite made a cogent observation when publicizing his memoirs. He reflected on how television began as entertainment and then grew into an institution of serious purpose. In recent years, allowed Cronkite, TV has reverted back to entertainment, and news reporting has become heavily dosed with celebrities and sensationalism. How else can one explain the morning-after decision by the NBC *Today* show to ignore the president's State of the Union speech in favor of two solid hours of rehash on the O. J. Simpson civil lawsuit verdict?

I, TOO, FOUND MYSELF PLAYING A BIT OF THE CELEBRITY game as governor of the far-off state of Idaho. I became a specialist at linking stars with endangered species. Robert Redford, a serious and committed conservationist, floated the Snake River to publicize our campaign to create a birds of prey sanctuary.

As fish runs on Idaho's Salmon River teetered on the brink of extinction, I was scheduled to release sockeye salmon into Redfish Lake. The hope was that they would migrate to the Pacific Ocean and come back again. I arrived at the remote lake to discover that actress Jamie Lee Curtis was on holiday nearby. We put her in a pair of hip boots and she joined me in releasing the salmon. It made for marvelous news shots. I took a razzing, but Jamie Lee Curtis makes for a far more eye-catching sight tipping over containers of fish than does any governor.

At the same time, however, I tried not to become an addicted player of the notoriety game, one of those politicians who seeks any and every way to get on television. I didn't need constant exposure, and was convinced it would turn people off anyway. The voters hired me to govern, not strut. I recalled that the most effective politician of twentieth-century America, Franklin D. Roosevelt, carefully portioned out his public appearances and waited to deliver speeches until the people genuinely wanted to know what he had to say.

One major challenge for politicians in recent years has been to stay out of jail. It's not that they're serving time; rather, they're using prisons as photo backdrops for declarations that they favor law 'n' order. Bob Dole even dropped in on San Quentin during the 1996 presidential campaign to promise tougher judges.

I came into office, during my second stint as governor, facing an unbearable population crunch in the state corrections system. We were housing state prisoners in county jails. I asked the Idaho Legislature for a new maximum-security prison, saying it was the one and only time I would make such a request. Henceforth, to reduce the population behind bars, we would study such punishments as twenty-four-hour home confinement for nonviolent offenders, or work to remunerate their victims.

The proposal did not go down easily. The American Civil Liberties Union had won a string of court victories to guarantee prisoners more space. It meant our 248-bed prison would cost eighty thousand dollars per bed. I gained approval of that prison without making a single TV appearance with guard towers and clanging doors in the background. It carried on its merits, and I made a point never to bring along a media entourage on prison inspections.

Some politicians are notorious for needing a constant "fix" of attention. While governor of Louisiana, Huey Long would march out onto the field with the band at halftime during Louisiana State University football games. A friend of mine once spied Senator Alfonse D'Amato among those waiting to board the Washington, D.C.–to–New York air shuttle. He shyly introduced himself and asked D'Amato a question. D'Amato beamed and boomed out the answer, obviously delighted at the opportunity to attract an audience. With little prompting, he kept talking as passengers boarded the plane, talked during the flight, and was still in full rhetorical flight as the plane emptied at LaGuardia. My friend was half-expecting D'Amato to get in the taxicab to continue his speech into midtown Manhattan.

I tried to pull back part of the time and recognize that, for a politician, silence can on occasion be golden. Overexposure breeds boredom, and often hostility. It's revealing that President Clinton's popularity ratings go *up* when he goes on vacation.

In my years as a cabinet officer in Washington, D.C., Sunday mornings were family time. I didn't jockey to get on *Meet the Press* or the other talking-head programs. My job was to run a department, master its budget, and advance its goals—not promote myself. I gladly traded TV exposure for an endgame assessment in the *Washington Post* that I was one of four Carter cabinet officers who had done an excellent job.

Television was never my exclusive means of communicating with citizens. One of the camera companies once aired a spot, featuring flamboyant tennis star Andre Agassi, in which Agassi delivered the message, "Image is everything." Not quite. Substance and performance still count, particularly when it comes to staying power. I did master certain tricks of the TV trade, such as looking into the camera and having the sun to my back so I wouldn't squint. In an age of shrinking sound bites it was obligatory that I learn to state my position concisely. My shortest bite was, however, about fifteen seconds.

Once, after a press conference in Portland while I was interior secretary, my old friend Tom McCall, former governor of Oregon, came up to me and said, "You're the best at using the medium that I've ever seen, with one exception." I was flattered that an old newscaster would utter such praise. I had to ask who ranked higher. "Ronald Reagan," he replied.

Still, TV is not kind to people who are bald and light-complexioned. I am both. Nor, in a larger sense, does it embrace somebody who takes a position out of conviction and then needs time to sell it. The tube needed augmenting. I continued to court newspaper writers who could explain complex issues. I wrote a political column for Idaho's weekly newspapers. And after delivering a televised state-of-the-state speech, I made sure to tour Idaho's Rotary and Lion's Clubs to deliver my proposals in person.

It was my good fortune, too, that I was able to gain a deeper understanding of TV by selling a product other than myself. I served in the early 1980s as a spokesman for the region's aluminum smelters and later, in both stints as governor, did a series of TV spots for Idaho potatoes. I wasn't paid to hawk spuds, and we insisted that the spots run outside of Idaho.

The campaigns each carried a message not easily boiled down to a minute, let alone thirty or fifteen seconds. Power rates were rising, but I was arguing that it was good to have an electricity-guzzling industry in the Northwest. The spuds spots made the case—absolutely true—that Idaho's climate produces potatoes of distinctive flavor.

From these experiences, I learned a bit about the tube's

demands. For one spot, I was plunked down in a kitchen, wearing a pink apron, and made to slice potatoes with a sharp knife while talking to the camera. Another spot used a cherry picker to plop me down on top of a pile of potatoes.

During my second stint as governor, in the late 1980s and early 1990s, I faced the task of finding a way to get coverage of complicated issues whose substance far outpaced their sex appeal.

I had decided to close off the U.S. Department of Energy's nuclear reservation, near Idaho Falls, to any additional shipments of out-of-state nuclear waste. For years, Idaho had been on the receiving end of radioactive garbage from the Rocky Flats arsenal near Denver, where the U.S. Department of Energy made trig-gering devices for nuclear warheads. The reason for prohibiting additional waste was concern for the Snake River aquifer, a great underground river that flows beneath the nuclear reservation and is a prime source of the state's water. We had a horrendous amount of the stuff already buried at the site. The federal govern-ment would make no commitments to remove waste that had been stored "temporarily" at the site.

I never believed in taking polls on what arguments would resonate with the voters. If I couldn't figure that out, I didn't belong in office. We struggled, however, to find a way of feeding the complex nuclear waste issue into a TV-dominated news machinery hungry for headlines. How would we gain support for our position and convince the feds we weren't kidding?

A newspaper gave us the needed opening. It was an instance of pure Andrus luck.

All shipments of out-of-state waste to Idaho had been banned by order of the governor. One rail car had made it over the border, however. The car sat forlornly on a siding in Blackfoot, Idaho, waiting to be sent back to Colorado. For safety purposes, and because I didn't trust the Department of Energy, I wanted a state trooper on duty twenty-four hours a day as long as the dangerous cargo was in Idaho.

A *New York Times* photographer just happened to be there. He lined up a picture showing the trooper, a guy with big biceps, with a patrol car behind him, appearing to block the path of the rail car.

The picture appeared above the fold on the front page of the *Times*. At some moments, image *is* everything. The photo let everybody know that Idaho's governor was serious about closing the borders. It woke up the Department of Energy. It sent TV crews scurrying to my door. The story was big enough that I was given time to explain the serious issue involved and the past promises that had been broken. I fed the headline hunt by hinting that I might place a National Guard tank on the tracks, with its muzzle pointed downwind.

Under the interstate commerce clause of the Constitution, I probably didn't have authority to block any railroad car. We never needed a legal test, however. The Department of Energy blinked. Governor Roy Romer of Colorado agreed to take back the waste. We signed a memorandum of understanding with the federal government, which gave us legal standing.

A FORMER HOST OF THE *VIEWPOINT* PROGRAM ON BOISE television, Sal Celeski, has talked about media coverage changing from "old-style think pieces" to "all-style headline bites." He has described me as a politician with one foot in each era. It may seem like an awkward posture, but it has worked to my benefit, particularly on coverage of conservation and the environment. The environment is one subject on which news coverage—even on TV—has increased in time and thoroughness over the last quarter-century. And, while complex, environmental issues serve up vivid images.

The Alaska congressional delegation has used every bit of its seniority and clout to increase logging in the Tongass National Forest. It has been a losing battle, however, because what they can't overcome is the ugliness of vast clear-cuts scarring Prince of Wales Island. The big pulp mills in Sitka and Ketchikan have closed, largely victims of public opinion in the states of the Lower 48.

As long ago as 1970, *Life* magazine nationalized the battle over Idaho's White Cloud Mountains, and displayed to the nation the place where the American Smelting & Refining Company wanted to put an open-pit molybdenum mine. Ordinary citizens were outraged, wrote letters to Congress, and let it be known that the White Clouds were a national treasure.

The occasion where I most intensely sought newspaper ink and TV clips came in the late 1970s, when I was interior secretary and we were fighting over how much land to protect in Alaska. It was controversial legislation. We needed a national constituency of support for the proposed parks, wildlife refuges, and wild rivers in order to counter the national lobbying clout of oil, mining, and timber companies.

Our solution was to educate the press and trust that they would tell our story to their readers and viewers. I could not verbally articulate the beauties of the Brooks Range or the fragility of the tundra, at least not enough to cause reporters to do stories. If they saw the Great Land with their own eyes, were able to feel it and touch it, they would write wonders.

So we scheduled a media trip. We weren't attempting to tell people what to write, only seeking to show off places that few had seen and that we sought to save. A big contingent signed up. Initially we didn't invite the *Anchorage Times*, whose publisher, Bob

Atwood, served as the voice of Alaska's log-it, mine-it, and drill-it boys. The *Times* had displayed outrageous bias on its news pages, and was fond of using such phrases as "self-admitted environmentalist" to describe people who disagreed with it. Years later, the newspaper would depict the *Exxon Valdez* oil spill as a boon to Alaska's economy.

Asked to explain why Anchorage's then-largest daily wasn't invited, my press secretary, Chris Carlson, delivered a tough-guy response: "We can play hardball too." A minor tempest ensued. We decided to let the *Times* come with us. Atwood dispatched a young, uptight reporter—not long out of military service—who initially acted as if we were the Donner Party and would come and devour him in the night.

The trip was a feast for the soul, featuring some of the world's highest mountain walls, greatest glaciers, and largest animal herds. We stood near the north end of the Bering Strait and examined relics of the Bering land bridge that brought civilization to North America. We reveled in the favorable coverage from the trip, but two episodes at the end demonstrated the ever-edgy relationship between a public official and a free press.

The party was scheduled on a boat tour of bird-nesting islands in the proposed Kenai Fjords National Park, near Seward. As befits an area with huge tidewater glaciers, however, Seward was socked in by a storm. We couldn't land a plane, so the interior secretary's press party headed south out of Anchorage in an ancient, groaning school bus.

What do you need for a five-hour drive with a bunch of reporters? Beer, that's what. I spotted a liquor store on the outskirts of Anchorage, had the bus pull over, and then took up a collection. Together with Joe, the state trooper assigned to our tour, I went in and emerged a few minutes later loaded down with bottled brew.

As I walked to the bus, however, the young man from the *Anchorage Times* raised his camera to photograph the scene. Another reporter tapped him on the arm and said quietly, "The picture you take may cause Andrus a bit of embarrassment. But it could get Joe in real trouble. He's on duty, after all, and he's carrying a bunch of beer. Let it go."

The guy lowered his camera. He had come to like us enough that he relinquished the chance to take a cheap shot. Later, when the ink-stained wretches bought Carlson a T-shirt with the inscription "We Can Play Hardball Too!" a two-dollar donation was forthcoming from the *Anchorage Times* reporter. I sure hope it showed up on his expense bill.

As Archie Bunker once said, you don't buy beer, you rent it. We needed a pit stop en route to Seward, and pulled off at the Portage Glacier viewpoint of the Chugach National Forest. The tour was taking place at a time when I was in a bureaucratic scrap with the Agriculture Department, trying to get the Forest Service moved under jurisdiction of my Interior Department. It made sense, I felt, to have management of major federal land-holdings combined in a single department of the government.

The Portage Glacier center had just closed, so eight male journalists went out into the trees. The young lady ranger inside heard the commotion and came outside to check its source. We had zipped up in time, but the beer-filled party had developed a considerable tailwind by this time. With whoops of glee, and one person whistling a few bars of "Hail to the Chief," the gang introduced this Forest Service employee to "your new boss." I was escorted in officially to capture the visitors center in the name of the Department of the Interior and put my name in the guest register.

My luck did not hold. One reporter took note of my invasion of the visitors center and my penchant for informally referring to senior officials of the Forest Service as "those bastards."

The top brass of the Forest Service in Washington, D.C., were not amused when they read his story. A distinct chill was in the air at meetings between the Interior and Agriculture Departments for sometime afterward. I attempted to apologize and blame the irresponsibility of the press. The Forest Service people suspected that the quote was accurate and represented my true view of them. They were, of course, right.

When it came to the fight over Alaska wildlands, however, the journalists' trip was a valuable insurance policy. It enlightened people in the Lower 48 who had never been to Admiralty Island or the Brooks Range. As owners of public lands, albeit far away, they were given reason to feel attached to these places. The journalists' stories introduced readers to resources and values other than the oil fields and gas wells that had hitherto dominated reporting on Alaska. Pieces appeared in the nation's major dailies along with a spread in *Newsweek*.

The trip so helped galvanize public opinion in support of preserving Alaska lands that a furious Ted Stevens hauled me before a Senate subcommittee to explain why the tour didn't constitute lobbying with public money. I patiently explained that it was an educational effort consistent with good public policy.

THE NEW SPIRIT OF *GOTCHA* IN JOURNALISM HAS extended down to the local level. It means an officeholder must forever be on guard. While I was governor, the publisher of the *Times-News* in Twin Falls, Idaho, wanted to be named to the state board of education. I didn't oblige him. He began to take personal shots at me whenever possible.

I went to a union picnic in Twin Falls one hot summer day.

The newspaper was on hand, and I jokingly asked if I would have to conceal my beer. The reporter and photographer reassured me. The next morning, there was a full-color picture of me holding a can of Budweiser. I sent off the picture with an amused note to beer-maker August Busch III in St. Louis.

The picture was a pinprick on my thick skin, and out of the ordinary. We had a tough but fair press corps in the Gem State. I had real difficulty only with one *Idaho Statesman* reporter who tried for years to link me to gamblers. There was no link, but his baseless claims led to a confrontation between the publisher and me.

Stories like that can get recycled. When I was interior secretary, Jack Anderson ran a couple of columns reporting the gambling charge. I went to a libel lawyer and laid out all the facts. He told me that it all came down to the need to prove "reckless disregard" and whether I could claim damage to my reputation. My reputation was still intact. What could I do?

I never felt it a valuable use of my time to spend early-morning hours, as Mario Cuomo was wont to do, calling up reporters and heatedly taking issue with their stories. A display of controlled fury is, however, occasionally appropriate and justified.

On the afternoon of the Teton Dam disaster in 1976, I flew over three towns wiped out by a wall of water. It was a sickening sight. My helicopter landed on the grounds of Ricks College in Rexburg. The press corps charged across the field. A Salt Lake City TV reporter got there first, thrust a microphone in my face, and wanted to know, "Governor, are you going to rebuild the dam?"

"That is the dumbest goddamned question I have ever heard," I replied. "If you don't get that microphone out of my face, I will jam it down your throat."

The disaster was treated with respect after that, and the

governor was given a little space. I gave the press, in turn, every bit of accurate information that reached me.

It was easier for me to get over the occasional angry exchange than for my wife and three daughters to take it all in stride. The female of the species is, by nature, very protective of family. And in politics nowadays, the family can sometimes find itself exploited or targeted.

We lived in a somewhat run-down state-owned governor's "mansion" during my first statehouse stint in the 1970s. It was too small, and an awkward place in which to entertain. Carol wanted to put in sliding glass doors so guests could walk out of the dining room and onto the patio. She saved from the household expense budget of one year, and took a little money out of the next year's budget.

I was shaving with my shirt off in an upstairs bathroom one morning when a guy with a camera walked onto the back lawn. I leaned out the window and yelled, "Hey, what are you doing?"

It was a photographer from the *Idaho Statesman*. He wanted to know what we were building. "It's going to be another bedroom," I shouted. "My wife is expecting."

The *Statesman* wisely didn't believe that part, but ran a somewhat nasty story indicating that Carol was shoveling out state money on a questionable improvement. She could not, and did not, laugh it off. And therein lies a lesson for anyone entering public life. Spouses and families have become fair game.

Carol ran into a wave of editorial criticism in the late 1980s when she was proposed as a corporate director of Morrison-Knudsen, the big Boise-based construction company. She, and she alone, decided to withdraw. Given the problems Bill Agee later encountered as CEO of the corporation, it was probably fortuitous. But it hurt her, deeply. I have learned a bit about my wife over forty-nine years of marriage. She is a person whose integrity is absolute. She is by nature frugal, as well as independent of judgment. It made me damned mad that one price of public service was seeing the bedrock virtues of my spouse called into question.

Attacking the family has become a kind of blood sport nowadays. Witness the radio talk hosts and warmup speakers at Republican rallies who specialize in petty, personal ridicule of Hillary Rodham Clinton.

I saw it getting under way during my Washington, D.C., tenure. Jimmy Carter came from a family of free spirits. One sister, Ruth Carter Stapleton, was a high-profile evangelist. When Rosalynn Carter banned hard liquor from the White House, the president's mother, Miss Lillian, would sneak a little bourbon onto the premises to have her nightcap. The press made light of their activities, although Carter was deeply offended when cartoonist Garry Trudeau in *Doonesbury* depicted the White House as a hillbilly shack.

Then there was Billy Carter, the president's good-ol'-boy brother. He started out as feature article fodder for reporters making the pilgrimage to Plains. The first brother was soon lending his name to an awful concoction called Billy Beer. He was a judge of the National Belly Flop Contest. The climax was an overture from Colonel Gadhafi, the dictator of Libya, who offered to pay Billy if he would come for a visit.

Jimmy Carter displayed an endless, Job-like patience toward his wayward sibling. Asked about Billy's escapades, he would respond with disavowal and gentle disapproval. The president would add, however, "Billy is my brother and I love him." It was the declaration of a humane person and a practicing Christian. The chattering classes of Washington, D.C., treated the declaration with disdain.

THE NEW TREND IN MEDIA, OF SIMPLIFIED NASTINESS
and communicating in sound bites, came home to Idaho in 1980
with Republican Steve Symms's campaign against twenty-four-
year incumbent Senator Frank Church. A politician of conscience
who took unpopular stands, Church was chewed at by attack-
style TV spots. He was targeted by an outfit called the National
Conservative Political Action Committee. Its organizer, a young
man named Terry Dolan, ran negative ads that punched out
Church for giving away "our" Panama Canal.

Symms had the ability to talk in headlines and use props. An
apple farmer, he had rocketed into public office by the gimmick
of taking a bite out of an apple and telling the TV cameras he
would do likewise to the federal government. He also could
exploit another disturbing aspect of the media's evolution. It was
perhaps put best in the early 1980s when an ambitious Georgia
congressman named Newt Gingrich gave advice to some young
conservative activists. "The number one fact about the media," he
said, "is they love fights. You have to give them confrontations."

The smears worked enough to give Church a narrow, heart-
breaking loss. I was convinced that sometime, somehow, the
right wing would try to come after me with a similar campaign.

Six years after Jimmy Carter and Frank Church lost their bids
for reelection, I again sought to be governor of Idaho. I won the
closest victory of my political career. In 1990, I ran for reelection
soon after vetoing the most restrictive anti-abortion bill to have
passed any legislature in the nation. In both elections, I was
attacked. But I fought back.

Awaiting incoming fire in the 1990 race, we adopted a kind
of Strategic Air Command approach to the threat of a right-wing
blitz. I hired Bob Squier, one of Washington, D.C.'s best political
admen. I told him to get some TV spots in the can that would
blast my prospective opponents and the forces behind them. We

would have them as a deterrent, there and ready to use, but avoid a first strike if at all possible. I would make the decision on whether to use the negative ads, and when.

Why not fire first? Because it would have damaged the positive image I had labored to create, using free media, for more than twenty years. Andrus was supposed to be a straight shooter and a stand-up guy. Andrus could be tough, but he wasn't dirty.

The nasty stuff was not needed. I kept winning and stayed popular to the end of my fourth term in the statehouse. The job of a state governor is not always a happy one. Expectations are higher and more immediate than with any other job in politics. Still, I left office with an approval rating of close to 70 percent.

The image problem that most vexed me was that of my state. The mainstream media has fed on the militias and wacko right-wing radio hosts to typecast parts of the Mountain West, particularly my state of Idaho. We have been maligned and mistreated in the national press as a refuge and promised land for racists, white supremacists, survivalists, and antigovernment extremists.

People magazine profiled retired Los Angeles police detective Mark Fuhrman, of O. J. Simpson trial fame, and his new good life in Sandpoint, Idaho. The magazine had previously profiled ex–Green Beret and fringe presidential candidate Bo Gritz at his compound near Kamiah, where Gritz vows he will not comply with any government land use codes. The greatest publicity, however, has attended the activities of Aryan Nation Church founder the Reverend Richard Butler at his compound near Hayden Lake. NBC News made a national story of his annual summer conclave to which other neo-Nazi and Ku Klux Klan extremists are invited. Butler himself has played on the Northwest connection. "This is white man's territory. It has a Nordic climate, it's a Nordic territory," he told an Idaho Public Television interviewer.

We were being typecast, both by the Reverend Butler and by NBC News. Butler's annual hate-a-thon attracts at most fifty followers. If this ragtag bunch calls itself the master race, I wonder what an inferior people must look like. In the twenty-four years since the Aryan Nation Church was founded, it has made almost no headway attracting converts in the "Nordic territory" of northern Idaho. The outfit represents at most one-one thousandth of one percent of the population.

The new, short attention span of the media rarely permits history to intrude on its headlines. Idaho was the first American state to elect a Jewish governor, my World War I–era predecessor Moses Alexander. As the Ku Klux Klan grew in the 1920s, Twin Falls was among the first cities in America to pass an anti-mask law. We have some of the nation's strongest laws against hate crimes.

Very much to its credit, the *New York Times* did give prominent treatment to a piece highlighting efforts by the Kootenai County Task Force on Human Relations to provide an antidote to the racist poison of the Reverend Butler. It depicted the cooperation of a Catholic priest, a Jewish businessman, and a Native American leader in countering a philosophy alien to the community's values and essential decency.

I WILL CONTINUE TO CHAFE AT SOME OF THE NEW maxims of media coverage—the seven-second sound bites, the trivial pursuits of Washington, D.C., the emphasis on conflict, and the out-of-touch, seemingly unchanging cast of the "commentocracy" that pontificates from the capital.

One of Congress's funniest speeches in recent years came from Republican Representative Henry Hyde of Illinois during debate over a proposed constitutional amendment to limit terms of members of Congress. Hyde noted that columnists Rowland Evans and Robert Novak are among the most vocal promoters of term limits. The most recent subscription come-on for their insider newsletter, however, boasts that Evans and Novak have a combined total of more than sixty years' experience covering Washington, D.C.

If the cup of media coverage is half empty, however, it's also half full. I am encouraged by some developments. The comprehensiveness of coverage by Idaho newspapers has shown consistent growth. The *Idaho Falls Post-Register* once campaigned relentlessly for Teton Dam while at the same time railing against big government. In recent years, however, it has become a national pacesetter on environmental coverage with investigative projects on the Endangered Species Act and (in conjunction with the *Lewiston Tribune*) the future of the Snake River.

I was able to get national coverage of the battle to save salmon in the Columbia and Snake Rivers. It was heartening to see a top-of-the-fold front-page story in the *New York Times* datelined Salmon, Idaho, and to have Cable News Network asking tough questions of Bonneville Power Administration bureaucrats in Portland.

While TV stations continued to shrink sound bites, I could still get time on an ever-improving public television network to speak and outline my program to the state. My state-of-the-state speeches before the legislature went out live on television, and entertained a few insomniacs on C-SPAN.

I adapted to the new trends, got my message out in the media, and avoided getting overexposed—except in the eyes of one bartender in distant Detroit.

The president of Mountain Bell, the telephone utility, was having a drink in the bar of his Motor City hotel to unbend after a long meeting. The TV set was on over the bar, and the evening news was about to come on. Just ahead of the news, however, up pops the governor of Idaho in an ad peddling his state's famous potatoes.

The bartender looked disgustedly at the screen and observed: "You'd think the state would pay that guy enough that he wouldn't have to moonlight."

Chapter 9

THE CONSCIENCE OF A CONSERVATIONIST

T HE OLD MINING TOWN OF WALLACE, Idaho, had a dual identity during my last visit. Its historic buildings were serving as a set for *Dante's Peak*, a Hollywood disaster epic that would do a brisk business at the box office despite a negative reaction by critics.

A make-believe Dante's Peak City Hall had been erected. Fake vines climbed up the town's high school, rechristened Dante's Peak High School. A fake on-ramp led to Interstate 90.

The makeover was designed for filming the movie's climactic eruption scene. An old mine tunnel in the middle of town would provide a backdrop for the reunion of its scientist hero with his new girlfriend. It seems to me that nearly every disaster movie, whether the subject is twisters or the spread of a deadly virus from Africa, ends with similarly rekindled fires of romance.

The people of Wallace wanted the volcano to smolder on forever. The movie's daily overhead ran to five hundred thousand dollars, manna from heaven in a remote northern Idaho valley that watched five thousand mining jobs disappear in the 1980s. In nearby Kellogg, the world's largest lead and zinc mine had shut down and been replaced by one of the nation's largest Superfund cleanup sites.

The survival of Wallace is largely the work of my friend Harry Magnuson, whose immigrant ancestors arrived in 1890 to work in the mines. Six years earlier, silver, lead, and zinc had been discovered in the valley east of Coeur d'Alene. For decades, the valley produced more silver than the rest of the nation combined.

In recent years, however, Harry Magnuson and his son Tom have been selling history, local color, winter and summer recreation, and a still-affordable retirement setting. He was bubbling over at how the 350 people from Universal Studios who were filming *Dante's Peak* had reacted to a remote mountain town.

"They'd walk up and down," said Harry, "and say to each other, 'I can't believe a place like this has not been discovered.'

And that's what we're looking for. People who want to get away from California. Or retire. Or do something with the computer."

In a tourism- or retirement- or computer-driven economy, many details of life will inevitably change. As a mining town, Wallace used to be home to the Northwest's last four whorehouses. "Five!" Harry Magnuson corrected me. They, too, were victims of the mining recession of the 1980s.

Northern Idaho will never again be such a reliable source of Democratic votes as it was when thousands of miners worked there. Years ago, people joked that if they arranged to be buried in certain northern Idaho counties, they would stay on the voter rolls and remain politically active after death. When early returns from southern Idaho had me trailing in my 1986 run for governor, I phoned Mike Mitchell, my manager in the Democratic stronghold of Nez Perce County, and told him I would have to make up the margin in his bailiwick. "How much do you need?" he boomed with a hint of mischief.

Not having a guaranteed victory margin in Nez Perce County may be one cost of Idaho's evolution, but evolution for the better. Idaho and the West have experienced an enormous economic transformation in recent years. Our mining and forest products industries have slumped, but then slightly rebounded. They will never again play their previous role as economic linchpins in the life of Idaho. We have, however, surged in other fields and at last found the kind of challenging, well-paying jobs that allow a state to hold on to its talented young people.

For example, the Idaho mining industry lost two thousand jobs between the mid-1980s and mid-1990s. In the same period, however, the state gained eight thousand high-technology jobs. Washington state saw about five thousand positions in the wood products industry disappear in the late 1980s and early 1990s, only to pick up three times that number of jobs in the software industry.

When I arrived in Boise as a rookie state senator in 1961, Ada County had just over 93,000 residents. The total had climbed to 112,000 by the time I was elected governor a decade later. Spurred by a technology boom—and jobs in semiconductor manufacturing that paid an average annual salary of nearly forty-seven thousand dollars—the county's population has soared to more than 200,000.

I watched from the capitol as the state grew by 15 percent in the early 1990s. Nearly 23,000 people moved into the state in 1994, my last year as governor. During out-of-state jaunts during my first term as governor, I would be asked, "What's the capital of Idaho? Des Moines?" That mistake wasn't being made in the 1990s. Where are these people arriving from? My daughter Tracy ran for mayor of Boise a couple of years back, and found California and New York to be the leading contributors of new Idahoans. I wasn't surprised.

Technology encourages them to come. The quality of life makes it impossible for them to leave. It has been said of executive recruitment by Boise Cascade, our largest timber company, that they have to drag 'em in but can't drive 'em out.

Why? Look around. I live in my state's largest city, but I can be hunting for ducks, geese, pheasants, and quail within forty-five minutes of home. I can catch brown or rainbow trout in the Boise River, which flows right through town. I can drive an hour to a more secluded stream, which will remain nameless. I can hunt elk within two hours of my home. Or I can take in top-drawer entertainment at the Morrison Center less than fifteen minutes from the house.

It is a life of multiple outdoor and indoor pleasures. It is affordable for young families and retirees. Its quality is a prime economic incentive in an age when, increasingly, people do business where their brain or computer is located and are not bound to a location or resource.

IN A 1996 STATEMENT, THIRTY-FOUR ECONOMISTS argued that the natural environment of the Pacific Northwest is of "tremendous economic value." They said the region's reputation as a somewhat unspoiled corner of America is a prime generator of jobs, incomes, and industrial diversification. The economists' paper, drawn up by Thomas Power, chairman of the economics department at the University of Montana, concluded: "Our natural landscapes no longer generate new jobs and incomes primarily by being warehouses from which loggers, farmers, fishermen, and miners extract commercial products. In today's world, these landscapes often may generate more new jobs and income by providing natural-resource amenities—water and air quality, recreational opportunities, scenic beauty, and the fish and wildlife—that make the Pacific Northwest an attractive place to live, work, and do business."

It's a mouthful, but I agree with most of Dr. Power's argument. The conservation decisions we undertook during the 1970s worked to further Idaho's prosperity. We set the stage by protecting the quality of life that people are moving in to enjoy.

As a case in point, at my urging, the state prevented Idaho Power from erecting a big, polluting, coal-fired power plant. Boise was just upwind from the proposed plant, which would have been built without scrubbers that keep pollutants out of the atmosphere. The capital has since grown out in the direction of the plant site. If the Pioneer Power Plant had been built, Boise would be a far less attractive place to live.

We also stopped Consolidated Hydro's plan to build a power plant along a stretch of the Payette River, just an hour's drive out of Boise, that provides dramatic white-water rafting and kayaking opportunities. The project would have virtually dried up the river for part of each day.

I could see the value of preserving the Payette every time I drove north from Boise to my cabin on Cascade Reservoir. The river has Class IV and Class V rapids. Unlike remote white-water locations, the river flows beside a highway. It has become a magnet for rafters from around the world. On this issue there could be no compromise: The Payette River was not to be diverted.

We safeguarded world-class wilderness tourism with the decision to protect Hells Canyon and to put 125 miles of the Salmon River in the Wild and Scenic Rivers system. I imposed one condition when Jimmy Carter asked me to serve as interior secretary. The president would have to come to Idaho and raft the middle fork of the Salmon River. An accomplished canoeist, Carter kept the promise.

I would, however, add a qualification to the environment-is-key-to-prosperity thesis. Resource industries that were my state's economic foundations—agriculture, forestry, and mining—remain major factors in the Northwest economy. They may be surpassed, but they should not be discounted.

Agriculture is a colossus that generates $2 billion worth of crops each year in our region. Wheat, apples, and potatoes are major contributors to the export-driven Northwest economy that President Clinton likes to celebrate as a model for the America of the twenty-first century. The timber cut in Idaho still runs at between 1.4 billion and 1.8 billion board feet a year. Most of the lead, silver, and zinc mines of Silver Valley may have shut down, but a different kind of mining produces phosphate fertilizers that are sold throughout the world.

My state's license plates reflect its changing economy. The "Famous Potatoes" slogan is still there. I was never so politically naive as to try to take it off. Beneath the tribute to spuds, however, is a new motto: "Scenic Idaho."

PERHAPS THE FUNNIEST POLITICAL BLOOPER IN
Northwest history came during a hearing when Senator Warren
Magnuson of Washington tried to silence an environmentalist
witness. With his notorious inability to remember names,
Maggie thundered: "We can't all go live at Walden Pond. Even
Walden only lived there two years." Like Yogi Berra, Magnuson
had a way of making sense even when his tongue played tricks on
him. Northwesterners are a privileged people surrounded by
envy. But we can't really partake of the region's quality of life
without a job. After leaving the Interior Department, I spent six
years in the private sector. I did some consulting, worked a bit in
the natural gas field, took several corporate directorships, and did
some work for the Wilderness Society.

In 1986, disproving F. Scott Fitzgerald's observation that
"there are no second acts in American lives," the voters sent me
back to the governor's office. The private-sector nest egg gave me
the financial security to serve eight more years as governor of
Idaho. Pay was never the prime attraction of the statehouse job,
though it did rise from $17,500 when I began my first stint as
governor in 1971 to $75,000 by the time I left in 1995.

My work in the early 1980s convinced me more than ever of
the value of a good business climate. Big business is not evil. The
enterprise or entrepreneur must be able to make a legitimate
profit. Otherwise, there will be no jobs to pass around. Nor will
there be money for the education, conservation, children's, and
health programs that make up the heart of the Democratic Party's
agenda. I guess, in the terminology of the times, that makes me a
"New Democrat" or "business Democrat." It strikes me, however,
as straightforward, non-trendy common sense.

At the same time, I have always believed in decent pay. A
state should recruit jobs that can support a family. I am appalled
whenever I read that some place in the South has delivered millions of dollars worth of concessions to land some poultry or

catfish processing plant that pays its workers rock-bottom wages and leaves them with stress injuries they can neither understand nor pronounce. I was proud to have helped persuade a Republican-run legislature, in 1990, to raise our state's minimum wage from $2.30 to $3.80 (and later $4.25) an hour.

I returned as governor after the 1986 election thanks to a late surge of votes from northern Idaho, at a time when the state's unemployment rate stood at 8.5 percent. We were still suffering aftereffects from the recession that hit mining and timber in the early 1980s. The state continued to lose its best and brightest young people. "Diversification" at the time still meant processing potatoes into french fries and sending Idaho cattle to in-state slaughterhouses.

We set out to recruit businesses in fields other than agriculture. I started by persuading Republican businessman Jim Hawkins to become director of the state Department of Commerce. The state scored immediate successes in its recruitment. We caught and were able to ride a number of trends. One was an exodus of professional people out of California. The Golden State seemed stricken with natural and manmade catastrophes. Another was the West's suddenly recognized status as a gateway to the Pacific Rim, the world's most dynamic, fastest-growing trade region.

It also cost less to do business in Idaho than in any other place west of the Mississippi River. People were looking for affordable places to live and work in the West. Even with sharp increases in the early 1990s, the average sales price of a single-family home in Boise was more than fifty thousand dollars below the tab for a similar house in Seattle, and lower than in such inland cities as Reno and Las Vegas.

By the late 1980s, Idaho led the country in percentage increase of manufacturing jobs. In 1989, our unemployment rate dipped to the lowest level in state history. I had occasion to point out such facts when *Newsweek* ran its article that identified us as part of an economically depressed "Appalachia West."

Hewlett-Packard was our first major high-tech recruit. The company gave the Boise area a pool of highly employable people versed in technology. The state capital soon acquired a new economic giant, Micron Technology, a computer chip manufacturer with a subsidiary that makes computers.

I'm still surprised at what is possible in a technology economy. Idaho had the sense, early on, to extend a sophisticated telecommunications system all the way up the Snake River valley to Yellowstone National Park. It has enabled 350 employees of Power Engineers, in the mountain town of Hailey near Sun Valley, to access a mainframe computer in Houston. The FBI has plunked down a major regional data center in Pocatello.

Our state's previously resource-driven economy also started to score in Pacific Rim trade. Between 1989 and 1992, the state's exports soared from $830 million to $1.2 billion. We were still shipping spuds, but now also machinery, computers, and electronics.

MY ONETIME LEGISLATIVE ALLY AND 1966 GUBERNA-torial adversary, Perry Swisher, has said of Idaho's boom and my contribution, "It was on his watch. He had the opportunity to screw it up. He didn't."

It's an observation worthy of pause and reflection. The Pacific Northwest and Mountain West are attractive places. They are selling themselves as locales for both business and leisure.

How, then, does a governor help an economy take off and prevent bumpy landings? The first thing you can do, particularly as a governor in the West, is to get in a plane, cross the Pacific Ocean, and get to know the Asia-Pacific markets and their movers.

My press secretaries were always challenged to come up with explanations of what I actually did during Asian trade missions. It was difficult to lay out something that was wrapped up in ritual and in the culture of our emerging trade partners.

Whatever its clout at home, any delegation of American businessmen will have trouble getting access to top-level officials in Asia-Pacific countries. The people in charge do, however, have enormous respect for the title of a high elected official or cabinet secretary. If you produce "the governor," you get access.

I discovered that in the 1970s when, on a trip to Tehran, I found myself in a private audience with the shah of Iran. I'll never forget the ornate palace rooms, fawning subordinates, and omnipresent bodyguards. I'll also remember a guy who didn't seem to give a damn about his own people. We came armed with proposals for water technology and irrigation of Iran's rural lands, which have a climate and rainfall not unlike those of Idaho's Snake River valley. The shah was interested in arms of a different nature. He delivered an endless geopolitical lecture about the "soft underbelly of Russia," the Soviet military threat, and his urgent need for the most modern jet fighter planes the United States could supply.

I also tried to get the shah to buy Idaho potatoes. There followed a bizarre discussion about how Iranians like small, round potatoes in their stew. My state's potato baron, J. R. Simplot, was along and had no patience for diplomatic niceties. "Jesus Christ, you've got a knife, don't you?" he asked a startled cabinet minister. "You can take it and slice the damned potato down to any size you want."

My second stint as governor featured a memorable trip to Taiwan. I opened an Idaho trade office and found myself courting Mr. Yu-Shiu Miao, chairman of the Taiwan Flour Millers Association, a major importer of grain and a major industrialist of the island nation.

Mr. Miao was unable to speak English, or perhaps feigned ignorance of the language. He relied on a bluff, hearty aide we called Big Brother. Big Brother was a man's man who loved to toast friendship, cooperation, all future business dealings, and anything else that let him lift a glass over his head. I had to keep up with the toasts or lose face. I was nursing a hangover by the end of the trip.

The Taiwanese paid us a reciprocal visit, for which we arranged a reception at the Owyhee Hotel in Boise. I went to the bartender with a generous tip and instructions. I was to get a martini on the first round of drinks, after which he was to fill my glass with soda water.

The lifting of glasses was soon under way. Big Brother downed four gins-on-the-rocks while I consumed one martini and three soda waters. He was soon blotto. I remained upright and wide awake. Subordinates were suitably impressed. "Boy, your governor can drink. Big Brother couldn't get out of bed this morning," my chief of staff was told the next day.

The Taiwanese delegation bought more Idaho wheat than any other place in the world. We toasted $16 million worth of new business on that trip. I hadn't screwed up.

ANOTHER VITAL STEP IN NOT SCREWING UP A STATE'S expansion is to make sure benefits are shared by the people who are already there. Idaho has a tradition of self-made entrepreneurs. J. R. Simplot left school as a teenager and built a business that now employs about thirteen thousand people. Joe Albertson was a farm boy who grew up to take on Safeway and build one of the West's great supermarket chains. Harry Morrison and Morris Knudsen were two guys with the Bureau of Reclamation who went into business together in Boise. They became part of the consortium that built Hoover Dam, and launched one of the nation's great engineering firms.

A bootstraps mythology has grown up around the lives of such people, several of whom were wonderfully celebrated during Idaho's 1990 centennial and the Idaho Public Television series *Proceeding on Through a Beautiful Country: A History of Idaho.*

Entrepreneurial drive is still essential. When nothing is ventured, nothing can be gained. But education and technical training are equally vital components of success in America's new technology economy. I kept hammering at the need for improved schools, and found a device for keeping some of Idaho's best young brains in Idaho.

In the late 1980s, such out-of-state schools as Stanford and the University of Washington were raiding our valedictorians. Around that time, a friend named John Givens had an idea for an annual Governor's Golf Tournament. It started out on a modest scale, with proceeds to the Mountain States Tumor Institute and a children's home. By 1989 we had resolved to use proceeds from the golf tournament to fund five twelve-thousand-dollar scholarships each year. The academic scholarships were to go to graduates of an Idaho high school who were going to attend an Idaho college or university.

We had 176 applicants for the initial set of scholarships. After the selections had been made, I bundled together applications from all the runners-up, sent them out to our universities and colleges, and then called the presidents and told them, "Go after these people."

They did. A total of 103 of the original 176 applicants chose to go to college in Idaho. In eight years, we gave out forty scholarships, but 801 applicants stayed in the state to attend institutions of higher learning. It was the kind of constructive, non-sexy, not very costly effort that has lasting results. The well-fed commentators of Washington, D.C., have a tendency to look down on something like this as a "bite-size" program. They ought to come out and take a look at it.

ANOTHER WAY TO AVOID SCREWING UP IS NOT TO BE stampeded into approving every proposed development that comes along. I find it amusing to hear some corporate bigdoms make the argument, "Government should be run like a business," but then yelp when a government leader asks properly hard-headed questions. How much is this going to cost? Do you have the proper financing? Where does it come from? Who are the deep pockets? What kind of impacts will there be on the surrounding area? What will be the cost to us?

We had a French businessman come to Idaho during my second stint as governor. He wanted to build a grandiose ski resort and three-thousand-unit development in the upper Payette River valley, not far from my weekend cabin on Cascade Reservoir. The super-resort would have doubled the population of the valley near McCall, one of Idaho's most popular (and venerable) mountain recreation areas.

The project, called ValBois, aroused the suspicion of Boise investor Peter Johnson, a former Bonneville Power administrator, who has a place at Payette Lake. Did the developer have money to complete his ambitious plans, he wondered? Where would the resort's customers come from? The closest major airport, in Boise, was more than 100 miles away.

Economics is more than an issue of value gained. It can be a question of value lost. If the developer made a mess and walked away, everybody in the valley would have lost. Groundwater near the proposed resort was only three feet below the surface. Hay isn't what makes money around McCall. It's the water quality in Payette Lake and Cascade Reservoir. If that is spoiled, the value of the property goes down.

ValBois needed both state and federal permits. We made sure that the Division of Environmental Quality insisted on a full environmental impact statement. Its preparation took two years, and our environmental experts found flaws. The development foundered. I breathed a sigh of relief for policy as well as personal reasons. As Tracy joked later, "My mother would have lain down in front of the bulldozers."

ONE IMPORTANT WAY TO KEEP FROM SCREWING UP A period of economic gain is to invest your popularity in clearing up uncertainties that might bring it to an end. I always saw my job, as governor and interior secretary, as getting issues resolved so the state, region, or nation could move on. This belief has thrust me into the middle of a host of wilderness and land use controversies. In these controversies, parties on both sides grew used to the words running together as I asked a basic question: "Tellmewhatyoureallyneed."

In some face-offs, fundamental choices had to be made. In the mid-1970s, the largest opportunity for wilderness preservation in the Lower 48 states was Idaho's fabled River of No Return region, the two million acres of rugged mountains, white-water rapids, and canyons flanking the Salmon River. The leaders of our state's timber industry tried to scale back the designated wilderness by a third when they chose to go after an area called the Chamberlin Basin.

The lumbermen picked a fight that they deserved to lose. "I'm going to hand you your head," I warned John Fery, chairman of Boise Cascade, as debate heated up.

Using a federal grant, the state prepared a movie about the River of No Return area and the Chamberlin Basin, narrated by entertainer Jack Jones. It was called *Here but Not There* and was shown on commercial TV stations and before every local chamber of commerce that would watch it. Public opinion swung in favor of protecting a full two million acres of the wild Salmon River country. The designation was guided into law by Idaho's great Senator Frank Church and later named for him.

I tried to play peacemaker in other fights. Given my conservationist bent, let me explain why I tried to make some allowances for the loggers, or at least give them a business environment of certainty in which to operate.

Timber is a big presence in small Northwest towns. Of course, the economies of some places are being transformed. It used to be, approaching Coeur d'Alene, Idaho, that you saw a mill. Now the view is dominated by the Coeur d'Alene resort's world-renowned golf course with its floating green, a destination that has keyed economic recovery and growth.

Other towns aren't so lucky. Idaho's unemployment rate came down, but I watched the jobless figures hover above 13 percent in Clearwater County, the place where I started my family as well as my political career. Just to the south, Grangeville lost 110 jobs when the Idapine Mill shut down. About 20 positions were regained when the mill was reconstituted and reopened, but many of the laid-off workers were still unemployed a year later.

Thirty years ago, a north Idaho mill owner named Dick Bennett gave five hundred dollars to my first campaign for governor. Don Samuelson beat me. Four years later, Bennett donated to Don Samuelson. I beat him. I wanted to meet somebody with the judgment to be on the losing side of two close gubernatorial races in a row. We became good friends and I came to understand Bennett's business a lot better.

Dick owns a mill in Elk City, Idaho, one of the most remote locales for an industrial enterprise anywhere in America. He does OK off Uncle Sam. The Forest Service pays most of the money for the roads that haul his logs to market. In another respect, however, the federal government has been driving him nuts. Bennett needs to plan his business and investments. In order to do so, he must have a supply of timber available and be able to count on a timetable of when to get logs to his mills. With timber sales being appealed, and a nervous Forest Service taking ever longer to render decisions, he's squeezed.

I did what I could with the state's badly neglected forest lands. We found that we could both raise the cut and put in tougher environmental standards on how logging was done. But the ultimate way out, for Bennett and others, was a final decision on how to divide up nine million acres of roadless national forest land across Idaho.

A resolution of what to do with this land, and permanent peace in the forests, may be asking too much. Joe Hinson, formerly of the Intermountain Forestry Association, an industry lobbying group, perceptively likens the West's forest battles to the debate over abortion. "It is value driven with no middle ground," Hinson laments.

In the past, lumbermen tended to want everything. They threatened shutdowns and economic devastation if they didn't get their way. The posturing dates back nearly sixty years. But they weren't able to stop creation of Olympic National Park, or North Cascades National Park, or the Lee Metcalf Wilderness in Montana, or our own Frank Church–River of No Return Wilderness.

The timber cut kept going up even as these lands were "locked up." Meanwhile, the public looked upon the spreading clear-cuts, particularly on private land, and turned pro-preservation. After years of crying wolf—loudly warning that each wilderness proposal would bring mill shutdowns and unemployment—industry was not believed when the beast finally appeared at the door.

Until the 1970s, long-excluded environmentalists simply wanted a place at the table. Nowadays, they want to eat the whole meal. The argument, not without some legitimacy, is that so much has already been cut that every still-pristine place must be preserved.

With a long series of wilderness successes under my belt—Idaho had 4 million acres under protection—I tried to solve the impasse over how much more wilderness my state should have. I went to GOP Senator James McClure and said, "If it's Andrus's wilderness proposal, Republicans will shoot it down. If it's a Republican proposal, Democrats and greens will kill it. We're leaders. Let's go shoulder-to-shoulder and try to get something through Congress."

We tried and we flat-out failed. The environmentalists cried that the plan we came up with didn't protect enough wilderness. The lumbermen complained that even if they let that much land go, conservationists were not of a mind to leave them alone. Dick Bennett told me he would go for twice as much wilderness protection as we proposed, but only if he had ironclad long-term assurances that the rest of the roadless land would be made available for timber sales.

Did I screw up by gambling political capital in an effort to work out the wilderness impasse? Not for a minute will I concede that point. I was elected to be governor of a whole state, not just the growing population centers and emerging parts of the economy. I had my start as a gyppo logger. Clearwater County mill workers first put me in the state senate. It was in the state's interests to get a fair settlement that would both protect more wilderness and give Dick Bennett an environment of certainty in which to operate.

But we were not able to put the controversy behind us, and nowadays the extremists are in full cry. For instance, some of the Northwest's Republican senators have undertaken a clumsy effort to restrict public participation and roll over environmental regulations. The public won't permit a rollback, and these elected officials should be smart enough to realize that. Instead of trying to curtail the right to appeal timber sales, Idaho Senator Larry Craig should work to see that provisions for stream protection and wildlife habitat are adhered to. In that way, appeals will founder and responsible cutting will go ahead.

Nor should past abuses be used to impose a death sentence on the present-day wood products industry. I was aghast at the Sierra Club's decision, after a referendum in which few of its members participated, to call for a halt to all logging in national forests. It is an extreme position. The reaction has been used to reelect such anti-environmental extremists as Representative Helen Chenoweth. It also ignores the fact that some timber firms are cleaning up their act.

Slimmed down, with an emphasis on processing logs into commercial products, the timber industry is still part of the Northwest's future. I'll give you one example. An Idaho wood products firm, TJ International, is part of the portfolio of the Parnassus Fund, a San Francisco mutual fund that invests only in socially and environmentally responsible corporations.

THE FINAL, AND FAR AND AWAY MOST IMPORTANT, element in not screwing up is for an officeholder—especially a governor—to think down the line into the not-too-distant future. Crises of the moment must not be all-consuming. Building for the next generation and leaving a legacy are essential to public service. This means getting out front and making the leap of faith that voters will trust your judgment. If they disagree, losing an election isn't the end of the world.

On the north coast of Oregon is a walk-in campground

amidst old-growth trees close to a spectacular coastline. The place is Oswald West State Park. Probably only a handful of visitors each year appreciate the park's namesake or even know his name.

Oswald West was a governor of Oregon more than seventy years ago. He served a single term but had the vision to put the magnificent beaches of the Oregon coast under public ownership. Who could have predicted the coast's present-day popularity, its role as a magnet for destination tourism, or its importance in attracting high-tech industries to the "Silicon Forest"?

My thoughts turn to another Oregon governor, my friend Tom McCall, who confronted and thwarted developers who tried to fence off parts of that public coastline. It was McCall who spearheaded Oregon's land use laws. Suffering from the cancer that would soon take his life, McCall summoned his remaining energies in the early 1980s to lead the successful campaign to defeat a statewide referendum that would have repealed his legacy. What a legacy it is! Cities have boundaries: Urban sprawl comes to an end. Oregon was spared the ugly, unplanned sprawl that gobbles up the Sonoran Desert around Phoenix and subdivides ranches in the front range of the Rockies outside Denver.

If Oswald West and Tom McCall in Oregon were preservers, Earl Warren was the great builder-governor of California.

Warren is best known as the chief justice of the Supreme Court who presided over landmark rulings that ended school segregation in America, expanded the rights of individuals, and limited the state's power to intrude in a person's private life. The other Warren legacy, however, is that this post–World War II Republican governor anticipated his state's explosive growth. He moved to provide for it by building highways, creating a world-class state university system, and expanding parks. It was Warren's infrastructure that sustained his state for more than two decades after President Eisenhower picked him as chief justice in 1954.

The lack of Warren-like vision, and his successors' failure to keep up and expand on his legacy, is part of the reason why 1.5 million native Californians left their state during the first half of the 1990s. A fair number settled in Idaho.

In Idaho, and increasingly in the West, being a conserver and acting as a builder go hand in hand. Holding on to the best of the past is a vital part of assuring a livable future.

The expression "quality of life" encompasses both first-rate schools and pristine trout streams. It means using the mind, and modern technology, to create a product that will be used half a world away. But it also involves appreciating a natural legacy that caused Wallace Stegner, in *The Sound of Mountain Water*, to write, "Something will have gone out of us as a people if we ever let the remaining wilderness be destroyed . . . because it was the challenge against which our character as a people was formed."

The West is still a work in progress. We need to shape that progress in a way that takes advantage of both our priceless natural setting and the opportunities of the emerging technology economy. We are all called not just to use and enjoy our part of the world, but to act as stewards in protecting and nurturing it.

Chapter 10

WESTERN
WASTELAND

I N TERMS OF GEOGRAPHY AND TOPOG-
raphy, landlocked Idaho would seem one of the world's least
probable places to put one of the most critical functions of
the United States Navy. For nearly five decades, however, the
Gem State has been a center of nuclear reactor research for the
Navy and the federal government. It has also been a disposal site
for the unwanted byproducts of nuclear weapons production and
nuclear-powered ships.

I've been dealing with nuclear waste since 1971, and will be
until the day I die. At times, some have likened my relationship
to the reactor test site—now called the Idaho National Engineering and Environmental Laboratory—to Captain Ahab and
the great white whale.

I see it in far less dramatic terms. From the beginning, I
posed three requests to those running the Idaho arm of America's
nuclear arsenal: Get radioactive garbage out of the ground in my
state. Find a way to solidify liquid nuclear waste, and then permanently dispose of it. And do not allow us to be made a resting
place for hot stuff from nuclear power plants and other out-of-
state sources. The Gem State is not a dump.

It has taken a long time to get action on this agenda. I
started putting pressure on nuclear managers as a 40-year-old
rookie governor. Under a deadline now in place, if I want to see
the last nuclear waste removed from Idaho, I must live to be
105 years old. I fully intend to: My dad is 92 years old and still
going strong.

The controversy over nuclear waste has put me in three roles.
I tried to play constructive critic during my first stint as governor
in the 1970s, receiving—and believing—promises of action from
the federal government. Since those pledges proved worthless, I
confronted the Department of Energy in the late 1980s. The state
of Idaho provoked a crisis by banning further waste shipments
from beyond Idaho's border. Nowadays, I find myself cooperating

with the Energy Department, even though I am far from satisfied with the state-federal agreement that provides for eventual removal of waste from the state. If the feds start missing deadlines, it will be back to confrontation.

The nuclear age settled in Idaho even before I did. In the late 1940s, the Atomic Energy Commission judged that the high desert and lava outcroppings in the eastern part of the state were a suitably remote place for nuclear reactor research and testing. An 893-square-mile reservation was created, west of Idaho Falls near the base of the Lost River Mountains.

The landlocked site saw development in 1953 of the prototype for the nuclear submarine *Nautilus*. Five years later, the Navy demonstrated the first large nuclear reactor to be put in a ship. Navy crews were trained at the Idaho site. One young naval officer stationed at the nuclear laboratory in the mid-1950s was Jimmy Carter.

The engineering laboratory also became a nucleus of the government's efforts to harness atomic energy for such peaceful uses as power production. One of Idaho's more unusual tourist attractions is the experimental breeder reactor that generated America's first usable kilowatts for the small town of Arco. They lit twelve light bulbs. I have one of them in my archives.

Since the time of the *Nautilus*, however, the Idaho National Engineering and Environmental Laboratory has served as the final resting place for the spent but still highly radioactive fuel cells from the Navy's nuclear ships. The nuclear reservation has also received trainloads of toxic and radioactive junk from the Rocky Flats, Colorado, plant, the compound near Denver that used to make the triggers for America's nuclear warheads.

"Remote" is in the eye of the beholder, as I have never ceased to remind the federal government's nuclear managers for the past twenty-six years. Eastern Idaho may seem sparsely populated by East Coast standards, but in Idaho terms it has good-sized communities.

A look at the map shows that the area is of prime—though unseen—importance to Idaho and the Pacific Northwest. The Big Lost and Little Lost Rivers disappear into the fractured basalt of the federal government's nuclear reservation. The waters of these and other streams move southwest at a rate of two to ten feet per day, directly beneath the nuclear test site. The Snake River aquifer holds as much water as Lake Erie. It is a major irrigator of Idaho croplands, and truly a lifeblood to our state. Waters from the aquifer reappear in the Snake River canyon at Thousand Springs, replenishing a river heavily diverted upstream by irrigators.

I am not a nuclear scientist, but I understood one point from the beginning: Radioactive garbage from the nuclear reservation in Idaho could not—*must not*—be allowed to come anywhere near the Snake River aquifer.

AS A NEWLY ELECTED GOVERNOR IN THE EARLY 1970S, I became curious about what was done with radioactive waste at the site. I discovered that my authority and standing vanished— as completely as both branches of the Lost River—the moment that I stepped foot on the federal reservation.

The site's managers and their superiors in Washington, D.C., had erected a rigid defense against all critical questions. The self-defense system was built under the Atomic Energy Commission and burnished under the Energy Research and Development Administration, the AEC's successor. It remained in place after management was taken over by the newly created Department of Energy in 1977.

When I made specific inquiries about what was going on at the site, the first line of defense was, "Well, that's top secret and you are not qualified to know what it is." Secrecy was broadly applied both to the making of nuclear weapons, which should be secret, and to the disposal of radioactive waste, which should not. The second major defense was bland and patronizing reassurance. When I raised the question of the aquifer, the response was that seven hundred feet of dry sand lay between nuclear garbage and the water table. There was no migration and no danger. I was assured the waste sites were thoroughly monitored. The reassurance was false: When I took office as governor, the Atomic Energy Commission did not have any monitoring stations at the site.

After a big snowstorm in eastern Idaho, site managers discovered that a plume of contamination had extended out from one injection well. The waste site wasn't diked in a way that would contain the spread of moisture through the soil. A heavy rain came down on top of the snow and washed contamination deeper into the ground.

The patronizing was amplified, at the Idaho site as well as the Hanford Reservation in eastern Washington, with a condescending set of comparisons. Repeatedly I was informed that I would get exposed to more radiation by taking a cross-country airplane flight, or skiing at Aspen, Colorado, than I would by living next to my state's nuclear reservation. The comparisons were tailored with an eye to the sensibilities of eastern Idaho, which is heavily Mormon. At Hanford, a more secular place, reporters were treated to the joke that more radiation was absorbed during a sex act than by working at or living near an atomic weapons plant.

Such comparisons evaporated on close examination. Sure, there was lots of safe ground at the Idaho laboratory, or Hanford, or Savannah River in South Carolina. But it was equally true that some places on these reservations were intensely radioactive, and that the stuff could pose great harm if it migrated off the reservation.

The Atomic Energy Commission and its successor agencies were perfectly aware of the dangers. They knew that airborne radiation respected no boundaries. In 1954, AEC employees scoured the lawn of a Richland, Washington, school looking for radioactive particles after a smokestack belched ruthenium into the air. The incident was kept secret until 1979, when it was revealed by the *Seattle Post-Intelligencer*. The AEC also made controlled releases of iodine 129—a highly radioactive isotope—into the atmosphere to study its patterns of movement. The residents of farming areas across the Columbia River from Hanford have experienced unusually high levels of certain cancers that are caused by exposure to radiation. It is not yet known what connection, if any, there is to the nearby nuclear reservation. Federal officials insisted for years that there was no connection.

In Idaho, one specter haunted me. What if nuclear waste—whatever its level of contamination—ever found its way into groundwater used for irrigation? Our state's agricultural economy would be in danger of a meltdown. After all, a near-catastrophe struck sales of Washington apples after CBS's *60 Minutes* aired a segment on Alar, a chemical once applied to burnish the shine on red Delicious apples. The CBS report carried questionable arguments that the substance could cause cancer among young children.

I could envision what would happen if any plume of radiation reached the Snake River aquifer. Congress would stage public hearings. Television cameras would carry the news into homes across America. People would hear conflicting claims. I could almost see a wickedly funny "hot potato" drawing, done at the expense of Idaho spuds, by Pat Oliphant, then the editorial cartoonist at the *Washington Star.*

The nuclear bureaucracy's final defense came in declaring its own competence. We know what we are doing, I was told; don't worry and we will take care of it.

IN THE EARLY 1970S, AS I BEGAN TO CONFRONT THIS issue, the Atomic Energy Commission was chaired by an outspoken woman, Dr. Dixy Lee Ray. She had been an associate professor of marine biology at the University of Washington and became a popular character in the Seattle area with a TV program that explained crustaceans to kids. Later, she would serve one tumultuous term as governor of Washington, thankfully not overlapping my tenure in the Idaho statehouse.

Dixy Lee Ray belonged to the most unyielding class of believers, the converted. In modulated but imperious tones, the product of years in the classroom as well as training as an actress in her youth, she fervently advocated the atom. She delighted in making such declarations as, "Nuclear wastes are not dumped. They are stored."

The Idaho site presented a far different reality. Starting in the 1950s, supposedly low-level plutonium and chemically contaminated wastes from Rocky Flats were simply put into boxes and piled into trenches in the desert. Nobody kept track of exactly what was being dumped.

At Hanford, across the border in Washington, liquid wastes with lower isotope concentrations were poured into trenches, as was contaminated water from the Hanford laundry. The stuff leached into the earth. Radioactivity showed up in the roots of tumbleweeds, which blew across the desert. Wasps used contaminated mud to build nests in the eaves of Hanford buildings. Radioactivity was even detected in coyote droppings.

The only insulation, in short, came from Mother Earth herself. The desert sites were considered safe, even if a great aquifer ran under one nuclear reservation and the Columbia River ran alongside the other. In Idaho, I learned such terms as "injection wells," into which waste was dumped with the assumption it would not migrate, and I was told that the Snake River aquifer was so large it would dilute anything that reached the water. I helped pour the concrete that plugged one such well so it would never again be used.

Other, hotter objects were not adequately stored. In the 1960s, the Idaho engineering laboratory experienced the only explosion in the U.S. nuclear industry's history. It killed three people. If anybody ever tells you the nuclear industry never killed anybody, they're dead wrong. Radioactive garbage from that episode, including an old Cadillac ambulance, was buried in the desert.

High-level nuclear waste was more carefully dealt with by the Navy. Still, the fact that it was stored in Idaho rankled me. A nuclear ship would be refueled, say at the Bremerton naval shipyard near Seattle, and the fuel cell would be shipped to a "remote" place. I counted about one hundred thousand Idaho citizens living near that "remote" site. It wasn't Seattle, but were they not entitled to the same protection as residents of the Emerald City?

I made a nuisance of myself in letters to the Atomic Energy Commission. Dixy Lee Ray came back with reassurance and a promise. Idaho had it in writing, an absolute promise from the federal government that nuclear waste would be out of the ground and out of our state by the end of the 1970s.

Nearly a quarter-century later, we know that the AEC had not the slightest idea how to move it or where to put it. The hot garbage is still in Idaho. Since Ray's promise, the federal government has attempted to move other wastes into Idaho. And, in an agreement it finally signed with the state, the U.S. Department of Energy has until the year 2035 to remove all radioactive waste from the Gem State on the condition that Idaho takes a thousand additional shipments of waste, which will be removed later, fifty-five years after the first pledge to remove it.

ONE FACT BECAME CLEAR IN MY DEALINGS WITH THE federal nuclear bureaucracy. Despite all their reassurances, and a quasi-religious faith in their technology, the feds rarely had a plan, a realistic timetable, or the management sense of how to get from Point A to Point B.

This was due, in part, to their priorities. Under the lash of Admiral Hyman Rickover, the goal of the nuclear Navy was to build ships. In the atmosphere of the Cold War, the objective was to build better bombs—particularly warheads that would fit into the nose cone of a missile and penetrate a silo in Russia.

Radioactive byproducts were given much lower priority. Downplaying potential dangers was an article of faith in the nuclear priesthood, even among those who were aiming the missiles at each other.

It certainly didn't help that the nation's nuclear reservations existed in an atmosphere hermetically sealed off from outside opinion. Constructive criticism—or legitimate worry about contamination of the Columbia River or Snake River aquifer—was not tolerated. If you did not get behind "the site" 100 percent, you were assumed to be the enemy.

Polls showed, for instance, that an overwhelming majority of Idaho residents did not want the nuclear reservation opened to additional waste, and had worries about radioactive garbage already coming into the state. In Idaho Falls, however, a brain-dead chamber of commerce was all for giving the federal government carte blanche. The attitude was, "We'll take anything." They received a big federal payroll at the cost of turning a blind eye to potential dangers. It strikes me as funny that the most conservative part of Idaho, from which I was always hearing denunciations of big government, exists on federal largesse.

Over in Washington state, the mayor of Richland told *USA Today* that the Hanford Reservation workers were not cut out to be "janitors." The site contains the largest volume of high-level radioactive waste of anyplace in the world. The waste may not have mattered to Richland's city fathers, but elsewhere in the Northwest its cleanup is viewed as a task of paramount importance.

When agencies malfunction, the federal government's answer is often to create a new bureaucracy. So it was at the start of the Carter administration as the country faced an energy shortage as well as increasing difficulties with all aspects of nuclear technology. The "fix" was to establish the Department of Energy.

I was secretary of the interior by this time, and spoke critically of the new cabinet agency. It was created at the insistence of James Schlesinger, a former defense secretary fired by Gerald Ford who had come to advise Jimmy Carter in the 1976 campaign. Although a good soldier after the decision was made, I harbored fears that the Department of Energy was cramming together too many incompatible functions, from building bombs to encouraging wind energy. The department would never become a cohesive whole or an effective agency. In the Northwest, for instance, it embraced a power-marketing agency—the Bonneville Power Administration—as well as two major nuclear weapons facilities.

WHEN I RETURNED TO THE IDAHO GOVERNOR'S OFFICE
in 1987, it was—to borrow Yogi Berra's famous phrase—déjà vu
all over again. The waste remained underground in the Idaho
desert. The federal government was still struggling to complete
something called the Waste Isolation Pilot Project (WIPP) in
New Mexico. It would replace "temporary" storage in Idaho and
become the final resting place for transuranic waste, the chemical and radioactive garbage generated by such facilities as
Rocky Flats.

The Department of Energy was also falling behind in establishment of a permanent high-level waste repository at Yucca
Flats in Nevada. About two million gallons of high-level liquid
waste were stored at the Idaho site.

On most occasions in life, it makes sense to give peace a
chance. At times, however, it becomes necessary to raise hell. The
nuclear waste situation had crossed that threshold. Our strategy
could be summed up as follows: Give yourself standing by taking
a stand.

Although storage conditions had improved, we were still
receiving and generating more radioactive materials all the time.
A Colorado utility was clamoring to use Idaho as a storage site for
waste from a commercial nuclear reactor. There was no indication
when it would end.

We had no date certain for when WIPP would become operational. I took a tour of the New Mexico site, and it was clear that
the site was a technically acceptable place to store transuranic
waste. But the Department of Energy could not even offer a
guesstimate as to when WIPP would start taking it. (The agency
is now giving a date simultaneous to the scheduled publication of
this book.)

The attitude problem had shifted locations, however. By the
late 1980s, there had been a transformation in outlook at the

Idaho site. Its managers were no longer stonewalling and patronizing but responsive, open, willing to talk and give straightforward answers. We had no such luck with senior brass at the Forrestal Building, the Department of Energy's headquarters in Washington, D.C.

I had learned one basic lesson as a cabinet secretary: The government in our nation's capital reacts only to crises. If we wanted action, we would have to create a crisis and force the Department of Energy to give us its attention.

The crisis had to be carefully calibrated. We could not, of course, block waste that was being generated by reactor research on the Idaho reservation itself. Nor would we be an impediment to national security. We would not stand in the way if the Navy really needed to ship us spent fuel cells from its ships. But officers with braids on their sleeves would have to convince this former enlisted man of that need.

The chosen target became radioactive waste from the nuclear weapons trigger factory at Rocky Flats in Colorado. Unless the Department of Energy gave us a date certain for operation of WIPP, we would turn back trains at the border.

I have related elsewhere our lucky break in 1988 of getting a prominent picture in the *New York Times* showing a patrol car and muscular state trooper sitting in front of a rail car filled with nuclear waste that had come from—and would soon be on its way back to—Colorado.

The picture conveyed a simple message: "You're going nowhere." Two positive consequences, one hoped-for and the other accidental, came from the publicized confrontation.

What we had hoped for happened. The Department of Energy became frightened that other states would follow our lead. If other places turned away out-of-state nuclear waste, those who generated it would have to keep it. The producers of waste included not only bomb factories but also universities and hospitals. Radioactive garbage would back up across the country. We provided a visible trigger to a complicated subject. By closing its borders, Idaho brought the whole issue of nuclear waste—and the federal government's poky progress—into the national spotlight. With its fear of a spreading rebellion, the Department of Energy was willing to talk. So were we, having poked the DOE in the eye and gotten its undivided attention.

Another branch of the federal government was not so obliging. The Navy reacted with belligerence toward hints that we would shut off its waste shipments unless there was action on high-level nuclear waste. Admiral Bruce DeMars, director of the Navy nuclear propulsion program and inheritor of Admiral Hyman Rickover's old job, warned that this would create a national emergency. Nonsense. They had barges on Puget Sound and at Norfolk, Virginia, where fuel cells could be stored.

Provoking a crisis was the easy part. It was far more difficult to hammer out agreements with the Department of Energy, and to get handles on legal enforcement and assurance that financial commitments would be met. We were doing the Lord's work, but with the help of lawyers. We signed agreements with the DOE to study transportation of wastes out of Idaho. But, when I left office some years later, the federal government was no closer to opening a repository, permanent or temporary.

The Rocky Flats situation had several twists. The Energy Department was operating under a state permit that capped the amount of waste that could be stored at the trigger plant. A Solomonic solution was agreed upon. Idaho would take any waste from Rocky Flats that was in excess of the cap. But the Department of Energy had to install a compactor that would keep Rocky Flats from reaching the waste cap.

Although cooled off a bit, the Cold War was still going on in the late 1980s. The Idaho National Engineering and Environmental Laboratory—the "environmental" part was added to its title in the early 1990s—was a booming place. Employment rose from 8,795 when I was elected in 1986 to nearly 14,000 five years later.

The site took the first steps toward removal of its forty-year legacy of radioactive garbage. In the early years of operation, nuclear reservation managers failed even to keep a manifest on many of the waste drums arriving from Rocky Flats. Now, in a far different political climate, the drums were inventoried. Some of the mixed radioactive and chemical waste was repackaged, assuring greater safety.

Of greatest encouragement was something called the Chem Plant at the Idaho laboratory, built by the Navy. It took high-level nuclear waste out of the blue pools where it was temporarily stored. Waste was reprocessed, calcinated, and encapsulated for eventual shipment out of state. It is a process in which you take high-level liquid waste, dry it, and turn it into a dry granulated substance that looks like kitty litter. The stuff is still contaminated, so you encapsulate it in ceramic or glass, and put that into a cask and ship it to a permanent repository.

As yet, there was no place for it to go. In 1987, after the Department of Energy had spent ten years in the fumbling quest for a permanent high-level storage site, Congress acted unilaterally and designated Yucca Mountain in Nevada as the final resting place for the nation's high-level nuclear garbage. For much of the following decade, however, the Energy Department demonstrated its legendary inability to move between Point A and Point B. The operation date for the repository, which would take Idaho's high-level waste, slid well into the twenty-first century. Only in the mid-1990s, under Dan Dreyfus—a former aide to Senator Henry Jackson—did site preparation achieve any semblance of direction and organization.

We had another problem: By 1990, the Cold War was over. It was good news for civilization. But it also caused the federal government to devote less money and attention to its nuclear reservations. Meanwhile, with advances in nuclear technology, a fuel cell could now last for the life of a Navy ship. Less high-level waste would be coming into Idaho; waste already there became a matter of less urgency. The Chem Plant was closed and employment at the Idaho national laboratory fell back to its 1987 levels.

The obvious solution was to negotiate a long-term agreement between the state and federal governments under which cleanup goals would be set and technologies mandated. Washington state had negotiated such an accord in 1989. The Energy Department had an incentive to be reasonable. Congress had at last gotten around to requiring that government agencies comply with federal laws on hazardous wastes. It mandated that the DOE come up with plans for mixed wastes and get states' approval for them.

I WAS LEAVING OFFICE BUT QUIETLY ENCOURAGED my successor, Governor Phil Batt, as he drafted a comprehensive proposal that was sent off to the Forrestal Building in August 1995. Two months later, without further input from me, Batt signed an agreement with the feds. I was traveling; my successor paged me at O'Hare Airport with a request that I sit down at a press conference with him and endorse the agreement.

I had taken a cursory look at the deal, and wasn't entirely happy. It allowed the Department of Energy to ship an additional sixty-five thousand cubic meters of Rocky Flats waste into Idaho. The tradeoff was that the DOE had to start shipping transuranic waste out of Idaho by the end of the decade.

The accord limited the amount of Navy waste we would accept, and prohibited the Idaho National Engineering and Environmental Laboratory from taking waste from nuclear power plants. The big deal, however, was that the government was required to build an evaporator by the fall of 1996, and begin reducing the volume of high-level liquid radioactive waste at the Idaho site. About two million gallons of the stuff are stored there, the source of my worst nightmares about the Snake River aquifer. All nuclear waste would be removed from the state of Idaho by the year 2035. If not, the federal government could be fined sixty thousand dollars a day.

In a line Ross Perot made famous, however, the devil's in the details. Our August draft had proposed shorter time frames to get stuff out of the ground and out of the state, as well as higher penalties for noncompliance. In the most important piece of fine print, we had proposed that fines automatically be taken off the top of the Department of Energy's budget. If it couldn't meet agreed-upon deadlines, the DOE would pay fines to Idaho before it could issue the Secretary of Energy's paycheck.

Under Batt's new deal, however, the Energy Department would have to go to Congress and ask for money to pay any fines. The distinction was important: Idaho would have a far weaker stick for enforcing any agreement.

The present and former governors of Idaho held an interesting conversation on the phone as I took the page at O'Hare.

"Phil, this document has a provision contrary to what we talked about," I told Batt.

"It does not!" he replied.

I quoted from page 13 of the agreement. The language was clear: If Congress didn't appropriate the money, there would be no fines or penalties if the Department of Energy didn't meet its deadlines.

When I got back to Boise, Phil Batt was on the phone again. "Yep, that language is in it," he said. What followed was a cussing out of lawyers that would cause some to blush.

The nuclear waste agreement gave me the opportunity, as an old political warhorse, to make everybody mad. I pointed out the deal's deficiencies to the press, which further activated Phil Batt's temper, which lately has never been far from the surface. But I refused to join an effort, led by some fellow Democrats, to mount a statewide initiative campaign that would wreck the agreement. Nuclear waste was, pardon the pun, too hot a subject for political opportunism. Let me explain why.

The deal negotiated by Phil Batt was better than no deal at all. The deadlines aren't as ambitious as I would like, but it accomplishes what has been my key goal for a quarter-century. The waste would be moved above ground, have liquids taken out of it, and be encapsulated. Better to have it in the form of kitty litter, and tightly protected, than sitting, as liquid, in the ground above the Snake River aquifer.

I believed Phil Batt when he told me that he did not know the provision for fines had been weakened. He should have known, he should have read the deal, and he should have caught it. But I respect the man and have known him a long time. We are of opposite political faiths, but he is a guy whose word you can take to the bank. Besides, the penalty provision doesn't come into effect for forty years. If we have a problem getting nuclear waste out of the ground and encapsulated, it will come well before the year 2035.

I've lately done some minor consulting for a major contractor at the site, which has provoked cries of "Sellout!" from those trying to undermine the agreement. What a crock! It should not be a crime to lend talents to making an agreement work. Nor does it make any sense to provoke another crisis when a solution has been put in place.

But I still reserve the right to raise hell. My role is that of a kind of human monitoring station on the Department of Energy's performance. I will be back on the hustings if the federal government welshes on any of the work it has committed to perform.

Chapter 11

Gone but
Not Forgotten

J UDGING BY OUTWARD APPEARANCES, the governor of Idaho seemed to be having the time of his life, joshing and arguing with farmers while drinking industrial-strength coffee on a crisp October morning at a cafe just outside the little north Idaho town of Potlatch. I was campaigning, but not for myself. The state had an open U.S. Senate seat in 1992, and I was trying to boost Democratic Representative Richard Stallings in his sputtering race against Boise Mayor Dirk Kempthorne, the Republican nominee.

Idaho politics have always been quick to change. As this book goes to press, Kempthorne is giving up a Senate career after one term to come home and seek the governor's chair that Phil Batt is surrendering after a single term. Mike Crapo, who replaced Stallings in the U.S. House when Stallings lost to Kempthorne, is now trying for Kempthorne's Senate seat. Stallings is attempting a comeback by trying to return to the House. If that sounds confusing, welcome to politics Idaho style.

In wheat farming country of the inland Northwest, give-and-take at corner cafes tests a politician's versatility—and competence. The conversation can begin with blue humor, but usually ends with complicated talk about currency values and agricultural export strategies of Argentina, Australia, and Canada. The Aussies and Canadians are competitors, for these farmers run export-dependent businesses. They boast computer systems that could operate the space shuttle.

Inwardly, though, I wasn't a happy camper. Stallings had disappeared into the back of the restaurant to call Bob Squier in Washington, D.C., in hopes that the Democrats' canniest media consultant had come up with a TV spot that would rescue him. "I wish he'd get off the damned phone," I said, in a remark that the reporter traveling with us would the next day have out on the *New York Times* wire.

It wasn't just that Stallings's campaign had stalled. I had memories of the great senators that Northwest states, including my own, had sent to Washington, D.C. Neither Stallings nor Kempthorne, a classic TV politician appearing to lack any rough-edge convictions, seemed at the time to measure up. My party was blowing an opportunity to pick up a Senate seat. Idaho seemed unlikely to send the next William Borah or Frank Church to the nation's capital.

Of course, every region of the country elects lousy governors from time to time, and sends less-than-sterling politicians to Capitol Hill. The Northwest, however, used to be a fertile breeding ground for visionaries, contrarians, and great dissenters. I fear that the tradition is being lost and that America loses something because of it. In 1996, for instance, a couple of the last distinctive politicians of the region retired.

One was Democratic Representative Pat Williams of Montana, who evoked the populist traditions of his state during nearly two decades in the House. Williams had the courage to point out that the great economic damage to Montana was not done by those wanting to protect wilderness areas. Rather, it was done by out-of-state timber companies like Champion International who clear-cut their land and then cleared out, and by East Coast mining companies that left open pits on the land and polluted some of North America's finest trout fishing streams.

The other noteworthy politician to retire was Republican Senator Mark Hatfield of Oregon, last of the Senate's great dissenters. As a governor in the mid-1960s, Hatfield was on the short end of a 49-1 vote by the National Governors' Association to endorse President Johnson's Vietnam War policies. Thirty years later, he was the lone Republican senator to vote against the balanced-budget constitutional amendment, which failed by one vote.

"Courage!" was the one-word slogan on Hatfield's posters

when he ran for the Senate in 1966, long before public opinion had turned against the war. Oregon was willing to have not one but two great dissenters in Congress's upper chamber. Senator Wayne Morse of Oregon had cast one of only two votes against the 1964 Gulf of Tonkin resolution, which gave Lyndon Johnson all the war-making authority he claimed to need. The roll of the Senate's early Vietnam War dissenters, or those with reservations that proved prescient, also included Frank Church from my state as well as Mike Mansfield and Lee Metcalf of Montana.

The tradition of independent judgment, and of flying in the face of conventional wisdom, began years before the Vietnam War. A Washington senator, Warren Magnuson, was probably the first to propose recognition and trade with "Red China" during the height of Joe McCarthy's who-lost-China crusade in the Senate.

The confounding of presidents by Northwest politicians has gone on for much of this century. William Borah of Idaho led the successful opposition to Woodrow Wilson's plan to have the United States join the League of Nations after World War I. Forty-five years later, Lyndon Johnson glared at Frank Church during a White House meeting on Vietnam and acidly noted that a previous Idaho senator had thought himself more informed on foreign policy than the president. Burton Wheeler of Montana was a down-the-line New Dealer, but he broke with Franklin D. Roosevelt to oppose and help block FDR's plan to pack the Supreme Court.

It was a Northwest politician who became the only member of Congress to vote against U.S. entry into both world wars. Representative Jeannette Rankin of Montana listened to FDR's "Day of Infamy" speech after Pearl Harbor and then cast the only vote against declaring war on Japan. Twenty-four years earlier, the former suffragette had voted against U.S. entry into World War I. And more than a quarter-century later, an eighty-eight-year-old

Jeannette Rankin would march at the head of a "Jeannette Rankin Brigade" in an anti-Vietnam War protest.

IF YOU WALK AROUND THE U.S. CAPITOL AND NEARBY congressional office buildings, you will see statues and busts of these people. Jeannette Rankin is there, papers in hand as if holding forth on a soapbox. William Borah is striking an orator's pose. A bust of Washington Senator Henry Jackson decorates an alcove in the Russell Building, and you almost expect his large head to turn and start giving an unending lecture on his latest preoccupation or fitness fad.

I came to know Jackson when he helped in my 1970 campaign for governor. He was a contrarian of a different kind. The dissents against the Johnson administration eventually became the conventional wisdom of the Democratic Party. Antiwar liberalism produced its own excesses, notably a tendency to blame America for just about every affliction in the world save for wheat rust.

Despite ambitions for the presidency, Jackson would not cut his conscience to fit the party's new fashion. He was an unrepentant Cold Warrior who spent forty years warning about the Russians' military might (and China's, until, on a Beijing visit, Jackson sat down with Premier Zhou Enlai and discovered that they had like views of the Moscow menace). He also believed in a doctrine I hope is not outmoded, that Americans should put aside their differences at the water's edge.

"Scoop," as he was known since newsboy days when he never missed a delivery, may have gone overboard on the subject of missiles, and as mentor to the Reagan administration's Richard Perle–style foreign policy ideologues. Clearly, however, history has vindicated Jackson's unyielding view of Soviet-style communism as a system that thwarted human initiative, brutalized peoples who wanted to observe their religious beliefs and cultural traditions, and despoiled the environment on a vast scale.

Jackson possessed another quality that put him on the honor roll of great Northwest politicians. It was an ability to see over the horizon and to stop incoming threats to the region.

I've spent much of my political career dealing with battles over use of water in the Columbia-Snake River system. It drains a vast area that encompasses parts of six states as well as great interior mountain ranges of British Columbia. Still, the river system cannot produce enough cubic feet of water for all of the tasks that man would have it perform.

It's hard to believe that, thirty years ago, bureaucrats in Washington, D.C., and water managers in the Southwest had their own furtive plans to take water from the river. The Bureau of Reclamation came up with what was called the Pacific Southwest Water Plan. Most attention focused on the proposal, later abandoned after a brilliant advertising assault by the Sierra Club, to put two dams into the Grand Canyon. However, the scheme also proposed to send water from the Trinity River in northern California all the way to Los Angeles.

The allocation formulas of the plan did not add up, however, unless water from the Columbia River could be diverted out of the Northwest and into the Colorado Basin. The plan made only a few oblique references to a need for additional water sources. Backstage, however, the Bureau of Reclamation was already working on the scheme and plotting to get Congress to authorize what would have been a gigantic siphoning of one region's resources for the benefit of another.

Jackson put a stop to it. He quietly inserted an amendment to a noncontroversial fish and wildlife bill that forbade BuRec from undertaking feasibility studies not approved in advance by

Congress. The Northwest's greatest river system was not even mentioned.

In his book *Cadillac Desert*, author Marc Reisner wrote: "The effect of the maneuver, which few recognized at first, was the same as if Jackson had strung a six-hundred-volt electrified fence along the entire south bank of the Columbia River. Without a feasibility study, the Bureau could not approach Congress for authorization. Without a Congressional authorization, it could not build."

Jackson's colleague Warren Magnuson also used what he referred to as a "little amendment" to stop an incoming threat to the maritime Northwest. The energy crisis of the early 1970s had put a premium on development of Alaska's Prudhoe Bay oil field. The pipeline to Valdez provided a mechanism for getting the oil on board tankers. What, however, was to be the oil's destination in the Lower 48?

The major oil companies had a place in mind. They were eyeing the northern end of Washington's beautiful Puget Sound. The area had four refineries. It could serve as the western terminus for a pipeline and be the site of a major petrochemical complex.

The plan would have meant oil supertankers plying the waters of Puget Sound. Oil-port locations were scouted, even still-wild Discovery Bay, where Captain George Vancouver's sloop anchored after sailing up the Strait of Juan de Fuca. The industry found an ally in Washington Governor Dixy Lee Ray, who discounted the danger and potential damage of oil spills, and rode the bridge of an ARCO tanker entering Puget Sound to prove her point.

But to most people, an oil spill was an appalling prospect. A spill would have catastrophic consequences for Puget Sound wildlife. *Seattle Post-Intelligencer* cartoonist Ray Collins depicted

Governor Ray hurling an oil-soaked duck into the air with the command, "Fly, damn you!"

The controversy came to a boil in the late 1970s while I was interior secretary. The Carter administration endorsed an alternative, the proposed Northern Tier Pipeline, which would have put the port well outside the waters of Puget Sound. Northern Tier's sponsors proposed to build a pipeline that would not only send Alaska oil to the upper Midwest, but also supply the four refineries and cut down on existing tanker traffic in the Sound.

In stepped Magnuson, quietly. He attached an amendment to a distantly related piece of legislation, the Marine Mammal Protection Act—an amendment that placed the waters of Puget Sound off limits to oil tankers of greater than 125,000 deadweight tons. A protégé of Maggie's in the Washington delegation, Representative Norm Dicks, guided the bill through the House.

It was done on the sly, behind the backs of oil company lobbyists, Governor Ray, and the Coast Guard admirals who could usually be counted on to lobby for the oil companies' point of view (anticipating future employment in the industry). Puget Sound was saved from becoming a Western version of Houston-Galveston.

Magnuson was a hero to most of the region, although Dixy Lee Ray called him a dictator. The only problem came as the senator explained his actions: Maggie was known as a man who liked his vodka as well as a man with a tendency toward verbal bloopers. Hence, Magnuson declared on a subsequent trip to the state, "I didn't see any need for these supertankers on Puget Sound. Why, the existing tankers can supply every distillery on the coast."

WHY DID THE NORTHWEST CONTRIBUTE PEOPLE OF such independence, foresight, and contrariness? I've joked that maybe it's the water. More likely, however, they were reflecting the region from which they came. We have always been an independent, contrarian part of the country. We dream big dreams, but we are fiercely protective of the resources and physical beauty that have attracted us to this part of the world.

It also seems to me that, when they moved west, people left a lot of excess baggage behind. They were more willing to vote for a candidate who was "different," be it in background or gender. They were willing to cut an officeholder some slack, and to back independence against those who sought to suppress it. Gender was less an obstacle. In the early 1960s, for example, the Northwest had four women in the House of Representatives and one of two women, Oregon's Maureen Neuberger, in the U.S. Senate. These were women who showed they could be every bit as tough as the guys. In the 1960 election, while I was getting my start in politics, Democratic Representative Gracie Pfost was challenging her male opponent to a logrolling contest at Lumberjack Days in northern Idaho. She dumped him in the water and, as former House colleague Ralph Harding told Idaho Public Television years later, "That finished off his campaign. Gracie proved that she was a better man than he was."

Alaska Governor Wally Hickel had just been named U.S. interior secretary in 1969 when, while meeting the press, a reporter asked if he had been able to sit down yet with Julia Butler Hansen.

"Who is Julia Butler Hansen?" asked Hickel, in words he would soon rue.

Representative Julia Butler Hansen, a Democrat from Washington, had been known as "the little old lady in loggers boots" since she entered that state's legislature in the late 1930s. She virtually ran the state Highway Department as chairman of the highways and bridges committee. Hansen would hold forth in an Olympia tavern, in the words of colleague Perry Woodall, "with her cigarette held at a jaunty angle." On roads, her word was law.

Later, as southwest Washington's congresswoman, she rose to chair the House Interior Appropriations Subcommittee. She held Hickel's purse strings. Colleagues had learned that visitors centers, road projects, and ranger stations disappeared out of the budget if they crossed her. Woe be unto a delegation member who forgot her birthday.

Hansen had retired to Cathlamet, Washington, by the time I reached the Interior Department. (She was still a power on roads, having been named to the state transportation commission.) In my political career, however, I owed a debt of gratitude to people like her. They taught the Northwest to appreciate a politician who spoke his—or her—mind. In turn, until recently, voters protected independent voices from the vengeance of ideologues.

Senator William Borah of my state was a great Republican progressive in the days before that was considered a contradiction in terms. He championed constitutional amendments that called for an income tax and for direct election of senators. Instinctively distrusting big business as well as big government, he was a trustbuster, an early critic of sweatshop textile mills in the South, and a supporter of a Department of Labor.

Borah was also a contrarian. As a young man he helped stop a lynch mob, but later in the Senate he was a key voice in the defeat of an anti-lynching bill. He saw it as an issue of states' rights. As with Magnuson on China three decades later, he endured criticism after an early call for recognition of the Soviet Union.

Richard Neuberger, the future Oregon senator, summed up Borah in his book *Our Promised Land*, published in 1938, two years before the senator's death. "What do trappers in the Sawtooth Range and boatmen on the Snake River know about the

World Court and states' rights and the sending of an ambassador to the Soviet Union?" asked Neuberger. "But they do recognize a forthright senator when they see him in action. The voters of Idaho are so devoted to Borah personally that they will accept utterances from him that might incite them to violence against someone else.

"In 1918 he condemned the espionage laws as drumhead government; he carried the state decisively that November. The same year [a woman named] Kate Richards O'Hare was forcibly thrown out of Twin Falls for saying almost the same thing."

In my time, Mike Mansfield and Frank Church were examples of politicians whose stands were not always agreed with, but whose judgment was trusted, as Borah's had been six decades earlier.

Mansfield is a shy, soft-spoken former college teacher whose academic specialty was the Far East. He was the antithesis of a suspender-snapping platform orator. But the miners and loggers and ranchers of Montana sent him to Congress for three decades, and fellow lawmakers made him Senate majority leader for sixteen years.

Church was Idaho's model for fearlessness. He was relentlessly attacked in his 1968 and 1974 reelection races because of his doubts about the Vietnam War. But he won decisively in both elections. The voters appreciated his meticulous attention to state issues and constituent work, but also had trust in the person.

In turn, Church treated his Senate seat not as a prize to be kept in a trophy case, but as a gift to be used for the public good. How else to explain why a senator from conservative Idaho would lead a probe into excesses of the Central Intelligence Agency? Or provide a decisive vote in ratifying the Panama Canal Treaty? Or move in and decide an emotion-charged wilderness controversy, on the eve of his most difficult reelection battle?

THE EXODUS OF NORTHWEST POLITICAL GIANTS BEGAN
in 1968, when a little-known Oregon legislator named Bob
Packwood unseated Wayne Morse. Mike Mansfield retired in
1976 (only to serve effectively, far into his eighties, as U.S.
ambassador to Japan). Four years later, Republican Steve Symms
beat Frank Church by an eyelash, and GOP nominee Slade
Gorton ended Warren Magnuson's thirty-six-year Senate career.
Henry Jackson died in 1983. House Speaker Tom Foley was
beaten in 1994, with huge spending against him by such out-of-
state lobbies as the National Rifle Association. He is now U.S.
ambassador to Japan. Hatfield retired in 1996.

It's a trend repeated around the country. Consider the exodus
from the Senate in the 1996 election. In addition to Hatfield, my
old Republican friend Al Simpson decided not to seek reelection
in Wyoming, and the sensible, level-headed Nancy Kassebaum
retired in Kansas. Democrats lost the likes of Sam Nunn and Bill
Bradley.

What is lost? I'd cite a couple of comparisons of performance.

Wayne Morse was a cantankerous, sometimes difficult per-
sonality, but nobody doubted that he called issues as he saw 'em
and rarely calculated the consequences. He left the Republican
Party by refusing to endorse the popular Dwight Eisenhower for
president. While defying Johnson on Vietnam, Morse was still
called on by LBJ to occasionally act as a labor mediator. It was
work that could engender hard feelings from unions.

Packwood, on the other hand, was a very different animal. In
twenty-seven years as a senator—three more than Morse's
tenure—he devoted himself to two fundamental missions. One
was the relentless pursuit of campaign cash. The second was
taking whatever stands would help him assemble the 51 percent
of the vote needed to win the next election.

He delivered performances worthy of the movie *Twister*,

hurtling across the political landscape in search of political contributions and votes. In one election cycle, Packwood could sound like John Muir. He celebrated the pristine virtues of Hells Canyon, and supported the strictest plan to preserve the Columbia River Gorge. On other occasions he was Paul Bunyan. In 1992, Packwood donned a plaid shirt and regaled loggers with denunciations of his former environmentalist allies. He likened defenders of old-growth forests to 1960s antiwar protesters, calling them destructive and unpatriotic.

Direct mailings were the mother's milk of Packwood's politics. Gloria Steinem solicited donations in one campaign by vouching for his credentials as a feminist supporter of abortion rights and population control. The senator seemed to imply, in mailings to supporters of Israel, that he was Jewish.

Packwood came to a tawdry end, dragged down by multiple allegations of sexual harassment, but he seemed to set ground rules for the modern business of politics: Stand for only one thing, reelection. Use your office to collect cash.

Look at an Idaho map and it's not hard to spot designations in which Frank Church (together with yours truly) played a decisive role. We were of different personalities, but we worked together to resolve disputes and save places. It involved delicate tradeoffs, as with creation of the Gospel Hump Wilderness Area north of the Salmon River. A scenic gem of the Gem State was protected. Left outside wilderness boundaries, however, were some forested areas coveted by national forest timber users.

We can do a fast forward to today's debate over the future of national forests. Idaho Senator Larry Craig speaks for the timber industry on Capitol Hill. He has proposed new legislation that would restrict appeals of national forest timber sales, and under certain conditions impose financial penalties on the appellants.

Drafted by one side, the bill has provoked a reaction from the other. A recent hearing in Coeur d'Alene turned into a shouting match. Craig was demagoguing before the loggers. A Spokane-based environmental group, the Inland Empire Public Lands Council, used Armageddon-style warnings to mobilize a big turnout of conservation activists.

The same sides, groups, and personalities squared off at a 1995 Senate hearing on reform of the Endangered Species Act. No progress on legislation came out of the Lewiston hearing. And Craig's one-sided forest management bill is not likely to make it through Congress. President Clinton would almost certainly veto it.

What we have, then, is posturing and noise-making when what is needed is an ability to work out society's compromises. Campaigning has gone negative. Sticking one's neck out is seen as a way to lose your head. Every vote or action is calibrated to the question, "How will this be used against me?" Fewer and fewer people go to work to solve problems. Frank Church was a solver. So was Henry Jackson. Warren Magnuson's little amendments led to giant achievements.

NOWADAYS, NOBODY SEEMS ABLE TO PLAY HONEST broker anymore. And, in an age of wedge issues and nasty TV spots, people are less willing to be the first out on the limb with a courageous stand that serves as a catalyst for rethinking an out-dated policy. A nasty partisanship has taken over, and deliberate polarizing seems to have become a preferred tactic in today's win-at-any-cost campaigning.

Back in the 1970s, the governors of Washington, Oregon, and Idaho jokingly referred to themselves as the Three Muske-teers. Dan Evans and Tom McCall were Republicans. I was a Democrat. We made a point of thinking regionally, however, and cooperated on a raft of issues.

We also pledged to come to each other's aid. Tom McCall

campaigned for my reelection in 1974, and Dan Evans—by then a U.S. senator—made an endorsement in my 1986 gubernatorial comeback. (The duties and obligations of a musketeer had to first be firmly explained to partisan young aides on Dan's staff.)

I endorsed Evans when he was appointed in 1983 to take Henry Jackson's seat in the Senate. He had the only feet anywhere near the size needed to fill Scoop's giant shoes. Evans defeated Democratic Representative Mike Lowry in a special election. Lowry went on to serve a term as Washington governor and never forgave me for being part of Democrats for Dan.

A few weeks after the 1983 Senate election, a letter arrived from Washington State Democratic Chairwoman Karen Marchioro. I was formally invited to depart from the Democratic Party because of my disloyalty in supporting Dan Evans. Supposedly this showed that I was not true to the principles of my party. I didn't know whether to laugh or cry, so I got mad. What was their authority to demand my departure? What command did they have on my loyalty? Above all, what did they think politics was about?

During my political career, I won elections with support from Republicans and Democrats, liberals and conservatives, plus lots of people who may have thought I was a knucklehead on one issue or another but looked at my overall record. It was, I felt, a mandate to show some independence and knock heads together when necessary.

We have nationalized our politics of late, even to the point of faxed "talking points" going out daily from Washington, D.C., to officeholders and radio talk show hosts. Single-issue groups have effectively drawn a bead on such tall targets as Tom Foley.

I hope, however, that we can somehow restore that tradition of Western independence, and that our people on Capitol Hill will feel free to look ahead without casting fearful glances back over their shoulders. We need more people deserving of a place in Statuary Hall at the U.S. Capitol. I'm hard put to think of any incumbent senator or congressman from the Northwest who belongs there.

Chapter 12

WE SHOULD NOT HAVE TO CARE SO MUCH, YOU AND I

WHEREVER I'VE GONE IN RECENT years, and whatever I have been doing, Alice Lake has come along with me. A large color picture of ten-thousand-foot summits of the Sawtooth Range, reflected in one of the world's most gorgeous mountain lakes, decorates my office. Taken by outstanding outdoor photographer Ernie Day, this photo of Alice Lake is a kind of Andrus denning symbol, a visual statement of the part of the world in which I want to be and of the happy fact that I am there.

Being governor of Idaho represented the limits of my ambition. It was a job that could be enjoyably done in an exceptional setting, and a job where an individual's efforts made a difference. The state capital is the kind of town where a governor's closest friends can be people who have little or nothing to do with politics.

The job of U.S. secretary of the interior, by contrast, was a duty. Washington, D.C., is, as John F. Kennedy noted, where the power lies, but it is also a town where the power game is all-consuming. When I released five peregrine falcons from the roof of the Interior Department building, I thought the act appropriate to a city where life is an unceasing duel of predators and prey.

I came to wonder how many of the capital's power crowd go fishing with their children or grandchildren. When Bruce Babbitt and another Sidwell Friends School parent took their sons camping in Shenandoah National Park, I bet it was the first time an interior secretary slept under the stars on public land since I left the department.

Frankly, I found the power game and atmosphere of the town false and rarefied, and I left the capital with a sour taste in my mouth. The last twenty-four hours of my tenure in the Carter administration were telling.

I had received a directive from the White House personnel office instructing all cabinet officers to deliver a letter of resignation as of the close of business on January 19, 1981, the eve of

Ronald Reagan's inaugural. I phoned and told them that I wasn't quitting unless the president of the United States instructed me to resign. The reason for my delaying tactic was that we were making a last-minute effort to protect five rivers in northern California. I needed time, and I didn't give a damn if the town was all atwitter at the new regime about to take over.

My solicitor's office had found a provision in law allowing the interior secretary to declare rivers wild and scenic. I had ordered an environmental impact statement on the proposed wild and scenic designation. We were challenged in court, and the issue went before the U.S. Ninth Circuit Court of Appeals.

Stubbornly still in office, on the evening of January 19 I was up at the White House, where Jimmy Carter was holding a farewell reception for cabinet officers and close associates. An emergency phone call came through: The Ninth Circuit had upheld my authority to designate those rivers.

I drove to the Interior Department building, on my last night as a federal official, and put my name to the papers that protected the American, Eel, Klamath, Smith, and Trinity Rivers. I stood around with senior staff and smiled. We had beaten the bastards at the eleventh hour. My successor, James Watt, later filed a suit to overturn the order on grounds that I was no longer interior secretary. He lost. I had legally been interior secretary until noon on January 20, 1981, the moment Reagan took the oath of office.

IF I WAS ON TOP OF THE WORLD THAT NIGHT, THE morning after Reagan's inaugural brought me back to earth. No longer would a car and driver take me to work. I drove to town through the regular morning gridlock in order to keep an appointment with Orval Hansen, formerly a Republican congressman from my state. I pulled into a parking lot and the attendant yelled at me, "Get out of here. Can't you see the sign? We're full." I had to back out onto a busy arterial. After finally finding a parking place, I emerged from the meeting to find a ticket on my windshield.

As Alice Roosevelt Longworth once put it, if you want to find a friend in Washington, D.C., get a dog. Once out of office, I sure felt that way. I generated a minor tempest by telling the *New York Times* that "the reason so many people live back here is they don't know any better." Still, a job offer in the capital awaited me, along with another in New York. I wasn't tempted: Lobbying held no appeal, and neither did life on the East Coast. It was time to go home. Carol and I set out for Boise, not knowing what we were going to do but knowing where we were going to do it.

It has been over sixteen years, and two more terms as governor, since we took that drive west across the country. I've tried never to spend more than one night in the nation's capital. It amazes me to observe some Northwest politicians—Seattle mayors are particularly afflicted—seizing every opportunity to visit Washington, D.C., and angle for a job there. Don't they appreciate God's country?

The real movement, however, has been in the other direction. The Pacific Northwest and the Mountain West have become "hot" in recent years. People are traveling here from the used-up portions of America, either for recreation or to relocate permanently.

Newsweek magazine published a cluster map showing where celebrities have built getaways in Montana. The Big Sky State has been celebrated in lovingly understated (*A River Runs Through It*) and loudly overblown (*Legends of the Fall*) Brad Pitt movies. John F. Kennedy, Jr., took his new bride on a Big Sky skiing vacation at New Year's.

The nation's new entertainment, communications, and technology moguls convene each year at Sun Valley, Idaho, to think, work deals, and pose for a group shot in *Vanity Fair*. The resort at Coeur d'Alene, in northern Idaho, has been discovered by such publications as *Conde Nast Traveler* and the *Los Angeles Times*. Visitors are flocking to what used to be a mill town. Then-House Speaker Tom Foley strolled into the lakeside hotel in the early 1990s to give a speech. He was nonplussed at the site of bronzed, carefree, rich teenagers strolling about with tennis rackets in hand. As a youth, Foley spent his summers in hundred-degree heat working at a Kaiser aluminum smelter near Spokane.

Oregon is a refuge for such prominent Californians as former *Los Angeles Times* publisher Otis Chandler. The high desert country around Bend has managed to become at once a retirement mecca, destination vacation area, and magnet for software firms and manufacturers of outdoor gear. Wyoming is the nation's least populous state but its northwest corner has become a bipartisan summer hangout, luring the vacationing Clintons as well as ex–Secretary of State James Baker, who owns a ranch there.

Seattle received a kind of beltway legitimacy when a Washington, D.C., media bigfoot, Michael Kinsley, relocated to the area to edit a Microsoft on-line magazine. He was soon gracing the cover of *Newsweek* and writing an article about buying outdoor clothing for *Conde Nast Traveler*. He lured other bigfeet like *New York Times* columnist Maureen Dowd, who demonstrated after a Seattle visit that she could write the same catty, superficial prose about Washington state as she does about Washington, D.C.

ALL OF THIS ATTENTION MAKES ME CONCERNED FOR Alice Lake, and for Idaho, and for all of the not-yet-crowded places between the Rocky Mountains and the Pacific Ocean. Is the West in danger of being loved to death?

Let's start in the high country. Alice Lake is reached by a

pretty stiff eight-mile hike that gains about three thousand vertical feet, with several unbridged stream crossings and lots of loose rocks. The lake is neither overrun nor overregulated; the Forest Service has not required permits or set up reservations or quotas, except for horse parties.

In contrast, the Enchantment Lakes of Washington state—a supreme beauty spot of the Cascade Range, reached by an even stiffer climb—has all of the above. Its trailhead is within a three-hour drive of more than two million people, and the seven-thousand-foot-high basin has become such a magnet for backpackers that the Forest Service has imposed stringent conditions. "Smokey Bear" has set a quota on visitors, and limits hikers to two nights in the area. Dates are reserved months in advance. A few spots are left to be scrambled over by those who show up in the early morning at the local ranger station.

After a ten-mile trek up to enjoy the freedom of the high country, you are likely to meet up with a ranger who will ask to see your permit. If the encounter takes place at Leprechaun Lake, you may have to endure a detailed explanation of how to operate the Forest Service's nearby experimental human waste composter.

Similar restrictions have come to four great rivers in Idaho. The number of rafters going down the middle fork of the Salmon River is strictly limited, and regulated by the carrying capacity of campsites along the river. Without the restrictions, of course, the riverbanks would become a pile of toilet paper from one end to the other.

A Seattle club, The Mountaineers, has for years put out a how-to book entitled *Mountaineering: The Freedom of the Hills*. The title used to be very much to the point. People did what they wanted in the backcountry. The Sierra Club put out a film in the early 1960s to promote establishment of a North Cascades National Park, showing the club's director, David Brower, and his kids on a trip to remote Park Creek Pass. The party camped at the pass, tethered horses to alpine trees, and cut boughs to build a fire.

Everything Brower did is now illegal in the national park he helped create. Camping is banned for three miles on either side of Park Creek Pass. Wood fires are verboten. Stiff fines await anybody who breaks out an ax. The hills are regulated with increasing vigor across the West. Quotas and reservations are the order of the day from the hike up Mount Whitney in California to Wonder Lake at the base of Alaska's Mount McKinley.

Alice Lake does not need that kind of management—yet. I've never warmed to putting a bossy bureaucracy in the backcountry. It's great to have hills that are still free, albeit to those who go gently on the land.

Signs of human impact closer to sea level are even more unsettling. The West is showing lots of concern about keeping its remote backcountry and wild rivers from being overrun. Similar attention is rarely given to management of areas feeling the pressures of habitation.

My daughter Tracy ran for mayor of Boise in the early 1990s at a time when the city's growth rate was 6 percent a year. The annual increase has since slowed to 3 percent, which is still plenty. Boise has not planned for growth, but has allowed itself to spread out piecemeal. Tracy wanted to install a level of management that would safeguard the city's attractiveness. She suggested a private land foundation to acquire open space for new parks. She proposed a transfer fee on students so new residents would shoulder part of the cost of new school buildings made necessary by their arrival.

Tracy also favored a foothills plan to regulate the building on slopes above the city. It does not require a rocket scientist to see the need for such a plan. Builders are pushing houses far up ridges around Boise. They cannot, however, develop small, steep canyons between the ridges. Cheatgrass and other flammable plants fill the draws, creating an intense fire danger.

Tracy was talking about reasonable stuff, not any imposition of know-it-all government. In losing the election, she made an unsettling discovery. While people were moving to Boise because of the quality of life, they seemed unwilling to pay the cost of maintaining it. Growth was making big changes while not paying for the roads and schools required to service it. The entire state of Idaho has a population less than one-eighth that of the nine million people who live in Los Angeles County. Still, the infrastructure of the Gem State is showing strains in fast-growing counties.

Coeur d'Alene's growth as a destination resort city is good news after the blows to timber and mining suffered during the 1980s. Employment and personal income are up, spectacularly. Less encouraging is the strip development along U.S. Highway 95 north of town and the traffic piling up around discount stores and shopping malls. The same could be said for U.S. Highway 2 in Monroe, Washington, or the same route as it passes through the Flathead Valley of Montana.

So what, you say: There can be no gains without pains. Who am I to talk when I as governor cajoled, wheedled, and twisted arms to make sure that everything from computer chips to door frames was manufactured in my state?

I am, however, also a grandfather. A new generation of fishing companions is growing up in the Andrus family. I want them to have jobs and careers, and I worked tirelessly in public office to expand such opportunities. But I also hope to pass on the pleasures, large and small, of growing up in an unspoiled place.

How? We need to undo some past damage. Under the aegis of all-growth-is-good boosters, much of the West has been sanitized of its wildness and wild creatures. Every river had to be "harnessed." Predators were poisoned or shot. Salmon runs were sacrificed to power development.

Of course, most of this can't be rolled back, but remedial

actions are possible. The federal government should buy and take down the salmon-destroying dams from the Elwha River on Washington's Olympic Peninsula. The Army Corps of Engineers should be forced to lower reservoirs and restore natural flows to the Snake River for at least part of each year. Federal and state agencies should protect wolves as they repopulate western Montana. The remaining old-growth trees of such heavily logged places as the Yaak River valley in northwest Montana should never be cut down.

I'VE RACKED MY BRAIN FOR A WIDER, OVERALL approach by which we can hold on to pleasures of the old, uncrowded life at a time when people are thronging to the West. I've heard the word "sustainability" frequently used. It's usually a code word for encouraging the kind of growth that will not do permanent damage to natural systems.

It's my opinion that we should extend sustainability to embrace protection not only of natural habitats but of the human environment of the West, which looks so attractive to those on the outside. We should be sustaining clean air, clean water, and wild places—but also small-town values, the ability to make a living from the land, civilized debate, and the ability to resolve problems at a local or regional level.

We should do everything possible to preserve the West's open spaces. By that I mean not just critical habitat for wildlife but places where families and kids can fish, roam in the woods, marvel at a tulip field, or visit a working farm. It is, of course, important that we safeguard remote desert canyons owned by the Bureau of Land Management. But such projects as the greenway along Interstate 90 in Washington will have immense, positive impact in a Puget Sound region expected to grow by 1.1 million people in the next quarter-century.

We should also try to sustain the West's traditional way of life, but not at the expense of those who lead it. With retirement havens and destination resorts springing up in once-remote places, working ranches are being devoured. I favor buying up development rights or granting tax breaks to those who don't put multiple homes on the range.

Incentives are the way to go. Forcing changes in behavior on unwilling people, while taxing them to death, won't work in the West. Such policies run against a value system rooted to individual freedom. If you take value from land, the owner should be compensated with money or, preferably, an exchange for other land.

In the last four years, Interior Secretary Bruce Babbitt has negotiated habitat conservation plans with California land developers and Northwest timber owners. In our region, the landowners have agreed to maintain a certain amount of "old" forest and to protect streams and wildlife migration corridors. They can go ahead with timber harvest on nonsensitive lands.

Babbitt has been attacked by the everybody-is-a-sellout-but-us faction of the environmental movement. Such criticism is counterproductive. If you want owners to keep land in timber, they have to cut a certain number of trees. If you want developers to be sensitive to endangered species, show them the option of reasonable compromise. Leave a wetland alone, and you can build at higher density on the bluffs overlooking the marsh. Otherwise, owners will simply deploy chainsaws and bulldozers the moment there is a hint of something worth preserving on their land.

Development should carry its own freight. In four terms as governor, I never bribed any manufacturer to come to Idaho. We sold the state as an attractive place to live and do business. We never lured a company by letting it off the hook on taxes or winking at environmental regulations. Instead we made improvements, notably to education, that enhanced Idaho's overall attractiveness.

Incoming industries should not be showered with corporate welfare. In the South, this has mainly served to lure low-wage jobs, and employers who pick up and move again when they can get the work done cheaper in the Third World.

Nor should developers, particularly the housing industry, be lifted from obligations to help pay for infrastructure made necessary by the subdivisions they build. For instance, an energy efficiency code may add some cost to new homes but helps avoid the need for new power plants that are expensive and polluting.

Bigness *is* best at times. The sprawl edging out from some Western cities is dominated by houses occupying lots of one, two, or five acres. It is a formula guaranteed to gobble up open spaces. Far preferable is to let a developer of proven sensitivity do the shaping. A parcel of land can be developed to cluster houses, set aside an area for services, and create walking and bike paths. Wetlands need not be harmed and riparian zones can be left alongside streams. Wildlife migration can be studied and corridors created for critters.

Unfortunately, some are blind to such positive tradeoffs. Witness the fate of a proposal, for both homes and preservation of open space and environmentally sensitive areas, made in the early 1990s by the Port Blakely Company for the eleven-hundred-acre site of its old lumber mill on Bainbridge Island, across the water from Seattle. Amazingly, not-in-my-backyard sentiment delayed the project so long that the company's patience was exhausted; the project's financial requirements became unacceptable, and its prospects turned uncertain. The eleven hundred acres are being split into twenty-acre lots.

In recent years, much noise has come from property rights advocates. The sound is amplified thanks to generous financial underpinnings provided by big agricultural, mining, and real estate interests. The "wise use" movement claims to be campaigning for the West's traditional values. But beneath the veneer of timber families and rugged miners, it is about unsustainable exploitation of resources and uncontrolled, runaway growth.

Given a clear choice, the region's people will support land use planning and efforts to rein in sprawl. Amidst a Republican sweep in 1994, Arizona voters rejected a radical property rights measure on the state ballot. It had carried the backing of then-Governor Fife Symington. A "takings" measure on Washington's 1995 ballot, lavishly financed by home builders and the Farm Bureau, would have gutted the state's growth management act. It lost in a landslide. Voters in several conservative areas of Washington used the 1996 election to toss out county commissioners who refused to draw up plans under the state act. It happened even in Chelan County, where the state's meanest militia group has operated on the political fringe.

WE NATURALLY RESIST HIGHER TAXES AND ARE overdosed on politicians railing about how much money the government spends. But sustaining the West requires investing in schools, transportation systems, parks, and recreation improvements needed by a growing population.

It is, as the old auto-transmission ad on television says, a case of pay me now or pay me later. Seattle-area voters turned down a rail rapid transit system in the late 1960s. What an act of folly. Three decades later, confronting some of the nation's worst traffic jams, they are paying through the nose for a more limited rail system that was once rejected. Portland had the smarts to put in a light rail system, and has reaped the rewards in a revitalized downtown, particularly at night, and the increased ability to channel and cluster growth.

Despite a proliferation of destination ski resorts, and the growth of weekend getaway spots to pamper overworked professionals, recreation in the West is sustained by public lands. We are doing a disgraceful job when it comes to keeping up campgrounds, trails, and ranger stations.

One reason a place like the Enchantment Lakes gets overrun is that the Forest Service no longer maintains hundreds of miles of trails in the Cascades, Selkirks, and Rockies. It is hinting that trails may be abandoned in the Sawtooth Mountains of Idaho. It is even talking about pulling pit toilets out of Hells Canyon.

I am amazed. Many of our trails, campgrounds, and lookouts were built during the Great Depression, when the country's economy was gasping for air. In a booming economy, sixty years later, why can't we afford to send a crew around to collect the garbage and spruce up a campground? Or have the budget to put trail crews in the backcountry?

In our national parks, too, visitations are going up, budgets are coming down, and maintenance is going to hell. Summer rangers are still living in trailers that date from when Dwight Eisenhower was in the White House. Visitors are using rest rooms built in the Kennedy administration, when park visitation was at one-third the present level. Many parks are staffed by fewer full-time rangers than thirty years ago.

Congress likes to pay for high-profile projects in our parks. The old lodge at Crater Lake was lovingly restored at great expense, and no detail was spared in the equally impressive job on Yellowstone Lake Lodge. North Cascades National Park has a new visitors center, while interpretive centers seem to duel with each other for attention on the road into the Mount St. Helens National Volcanic Area.

It's impossible, I guess, to cut a ribbon around a newly hired ranger, or to make a dedication ceremony out of repairs to a New Frontier–vintage septic system. But there's a desperate need to provide for the unheroic requirements of our parks and recreation lands around the West.

AS I HEAD INTO THE TWILIGHT OF A LONG POLITICAL career, this old warhorse has a few other hopes. The first is that we attempt to think and act regionally. Some say, as Tip O'Neill did, that all politics is local. Others say to think globally, but act locally. I feel we must think and act regionally, in the Pacific Northwest as well as the Pacific Southwest.

I've watched recently as politicians like Washington Representative George Nethercutt tried to kill, and then to suppress, a sweeping study of the environment and land management in the upper Columbia River basin. The project has looked at 144 million acres of land in seven states, all of it drained by the master river system of the Northwest. It aims to provide a comprehensive picture of environmental quality and its degradation. The good sense of doing so is self-evident. We could deal with species before triggering stringent provisions of the Endangered Species Act. Communities would have more warning about coming changes to the timber harvest. There would be fewer lawsuits challenging logging, mining, and grazing based on the claim of not enough scientific information.

Some Northwest lawmakers have viewed the study as a plot to decrease grazing, logging, and mining on public lands while threatening private property rights. It's an attitude that reminds me of officials in the Middle Ages who tried to prevent anyone from questioning the accepted wisdom that the world was flat.

If the Northwest cannot sustain past levels of logging and grazing, or if parts of the landscape are threatened with lasting environmental damage, let us learn what the region can live with. Let us face and deal with problems—from lodgepole and ponderosa pine forests threatened with catastrophic fires to bull trout facing extinction—before we are in crises. A political solution is preferable to a judge's injunction.

My second hope is that the future of the West gets debated in a way that is rational and constructive. The public responds to positive messages much better than to attack ads. Public debate is not war; it's a marketplace of ideas that must compete for public support.

In my last term as governor, I tried to play referee in a battle between the Air Force and national environmental organizations. Mountain Home Air Force Base wanted to formally establish a training range for aircraft of more than one million acres along Idaho's upper Owyhee River. The Air Force already had, and still has, a right to fly over the area. The environmentalists fastened onto the proposed range and complained that earsplitting noise would disrupt bighorn sheep.

I stepped in with a plan to limit the training range to less than one-tenth of what the Air Force wanted. We would keep aircraft away from canyons where the sheep live. The environmentalists responded by turning their ire on me. They accused me of wanting to bomb the bighorns. They captured the ear of the Clinton administration and used the press to portray me as that most nefarious of villains, the sellout.

It made me mad, but also left me saddened. The environmental groups were, with but the slightest hesitation, willing to demonize an old ally. The battle was more important than the issue. It became a vehicle for raising money and recruiting members. Exaggeration, a basic tactic of politics, had become gross exaggeration.

We see equal or greater excess from the other side; witness a recent diatribe against "environmental extremists" by Perry Pendley, an attorney for the Mountain States Legal Foundation. "In their vision," he declared, "everything from the 100th meridian to the Cascade Range becomes a vast park through which they might drive, drinking their Perrier and munching their organic chips, staying occasionally in the bed-and-breakfast operations into which the homes of Westerners have been turned, with those Westerners who remain fluffing duvets and pouring cappuccino."

Laugh if you wish, but this is one blunt-spoken old politician who believes that language can be put to more constructive use. We can joust, and even fight at times, but it must be from a position of mutual respect. The issues are too important. The West is too precious to be used as a scorched-earth, all-or-nothing battleground.

Robert Frost once wrote, "We should not have to care so much, you and I." But we do care, and we should. We care about the future of our region, and I am thankful to have been given the opportunity to care about Idaho, and Alaska, and the West and its people, for as long as I have.

I remain hopeful that I will be able to pass on to my grandchildren all the pleasures of life in an unspoiled West. Perhaps hope should be replaced by a stronger word. It is a matter of obligation.

INDEX

A

Abbey, Edward, 48
Abortion issues, 36, 137–49
    anti-abortion groups, 137, 140–41, 147
Admiralty Island, Alaska, 75–76, 81,
    130–31, 161
Agee, Bill, 163
Agriculture and irrigation, 24, 48–49, 125,
    175
    nuclear waste danger, 193, 195–96
Alaska
    Admiralty Island National Monument,
      75–76
    Alaska Lands Act, 1980, 47, 67, 70, 76,
      78–81, 84, 131
    Arctic National Wildlife Refuge,
      69–70, 78–79, 122
    Brooks Range, 68, 74, 76, 84, 158
    development issues, 68–74, 76, 79
    environmental concerns, 67–70
    Gates of the Arctic National Park, 68,
      76, 81
    Glacier Bay National Park, 116
    Kenai Fjords National Park, 75, 159
    land claims, background, 71–73
    Misty Fjords, 68, 74, 79
    Tongass National Forest, 130, 158
Alaska Native Claims Settlement Act, 1971,
    72–73
Alaska oil
    and Arctic National Wildlife Refuge,
      69–70, 122
    pipelines, tankers, ports, 49, 69–70, 71,
      122, 159, 214–15
Alslager, Rick, 94
Aluminum industry, 88, 94, 99
Anderson, Governor Forrest, 32
Anderson, Jack, 42, 162
Andrus, Carol, 1, 29, 30, 36, 50, 116,
    163–64
Andrus, Cecil
    allies, friends, enemies, 12, 209–18,
      221–22
    Birds of Prey Natural Area, 113–16, 152
    business climate strategies, philosophy,
      23, 176–89
    campaigning activities, philosophy,

      11–12, 19–20, 55–58
    Capitol-for-a-Day program, 55–58
    Carol and family, 1, 6, 12, 17, 35–36,
      147, 163, 227
    educational support, funding, 10–11,
      16–18, 20–21, 145, 181–82
    elk hunting accident, 36–39
    environmental conservation activities, 2,
      4–6, 18–19, 58–59
    environmental preservation philosophy,
      5, 59–60, 68, 71–72, 81, 88–90,
      121–24, 129, 231–33
    governing ethics, strategies, 18–24, 25,
      27, 29–30, 35–36, 39, 41, 54–55,
      125, 154–55
    governor of Idaho. *See* Governor of Idaho
    media strategies, 22, 60–62, 152–61,
      162, 165–66, 168, 183–84
    nuclear waste disposal fight, 61–62,
      191–207
    Pioneer power plant, 62–63, 174
    political action, strategies, 7, 20–25,
      50–55, 58–62, 132, 142, 152–53, 233
    private sector years, 88, 115, 176
    public service principles, 51–54, 176,
      180, 182–83, 187
    salmon preservation efforts, 87–111. *See
      also* Salmon
    secretary, department of the interior, 1,
      35, 47–50, 54, 67–74, 78–81,
      179–80, 225
    Wild and Scenic River protection,
      225–26
    work and strategies, past and future,
      225–39
    working with President Carter, 48–50,
      53, 67–68, 71, 83–84
    youth, background, 1, 2, 7, 9, 11, 35,
      45, 81, 87
Andrus, Tracy, 36, 147, 173, 230–31
Army Corps of Engineers, 5, 87
    history, public accountability, 97–98,
      100–01
    policies, 5, 89, 97, 99, 103
    resistance to salmon preservation, 5–6,
      99–106
    salmon preservation study, 107–08. *See
      also* Dams
Atomic Energy Commission, 61, 192–93,
    195–97
Atwood, Bob, 158–59